Fascinating
Tampa Bay
TRIVIA

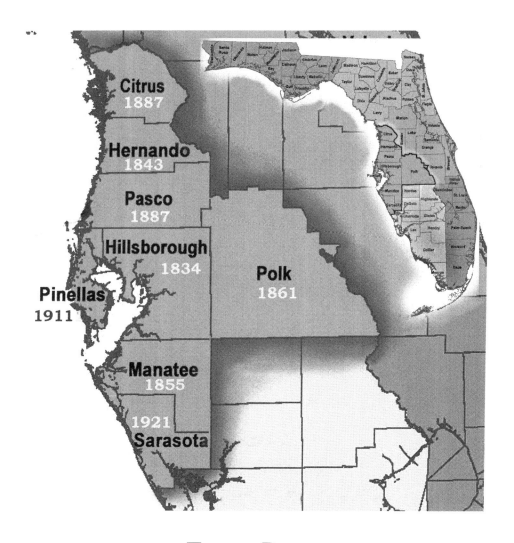

Tampa Bay

This map shows the eight counties that make up the Tampa Bay Region covered in this volume.

It also shows the area in relation to the state (inset map) and the year each of the counties in the *Tampa Bay Region* was formed.

Fascinating Tampa Bay TRIVIA

Compiled by

Robert A. Powell

Silverhawke Publications

Published & Distributed by

Silverhawke Publications

Bayonet Point, Florida 34667

ISBN 978-1497481329

Copyright 2012 by Robert A. Powell

Fascinating Trivia

• *Tampa Bay* area was once a home to various native American cultures, including the *Tocobaga* and the *Calusa*.

• The modern history for *Tampa* began in 1823, with the founding of **Fort Brooke** in today's downtown. Growth came slowly for the small village during its first half-century, due to poor transportation, conflicts with the Seminole tribe, and repeated outbreaks of yellow fever.

• In the 1880s the railroad and new industries brought sudden prosperity and attracted many new residents to *Tampa*. By the turn of the 19th century, *Tampa* had grown into one of the largest cities in *Florida*, a status it has kept ever since.

• The origin of the name *"Tampa"* is not documented. It means "sticks of fire" in the language of the *Calusa*, a Native American tribe that once lived in the area. Most historians think they called it "sticks of fire" for the high number of lightning strikes *Tampa Bay* receives yearly. Some other historians claim the name merely refers to "the place to gather sticks" for their campfire.

The old cannon from Fort Brooke is now a part of the Plant Park on the campus of the **University of Tampa**.

• The name *Tampa* appears in the 1575 memoir of *Hernando de Escalante Fontaneda,* who spent 17 years as a *Calusa* captive. He calls it *"Tanpa"* and describes it as an important *Calusa* town. Noted archaeologist **Jerald Milanich** places the *Calusa* village of *Tanpa* at the mouth of *Charlotte Harbor.* A later Spanish expedition accidentally transferred the name north to present-day *Tampa Bay.*

- *Tampa* was an embarkation center for American troops in the *Spanish-American War. Lt. Colonel Teddy Roosevelt* and his *Rough Riders* were among 30,000 troops who waited in *Tampa* for the order to ship out to Cuba in 1898.

- *Great Britain* acquired Florida in 1763 as part of the treaty to end the *French and Indian War. Tampa Bay* was renamed *Hillsborough Bay*, after Lord Hillsborough, Secretary of State for the Colonies. His name adorns Tampa's largest river and county. *Britain* was more concerned with the strategic *Atlantic* coast of *Florida* than the mostly empty *Gulf* coast, and the *Tampa* area was virtually disregarded.

Lt. Col. Teddy Roosevelt 1898 in Tampa - waiting to leave for "San Juan Hill" with his Rough Riders. Spanish American War

- The original native population died out from European-spread disease introduced by early expeditions. The *Seminoles* living to the north, were seasonal residents of *Tampa Bay*, as well as Cuban fishermen, who stayed in temporary settlements along today's Bayshore Boulevard. They would catch a large haul of fish, and take them back to sell in Cuba.

- Transportation magnate *Henry B. Plant* extended his railroad line to *Tampa* and its port in the 1880s, connecting the small town to the country's vast railroad system. This important transportation link allowed phosphate and commercial fishing exports to go north, as well as bringing new products into the Tampa market, and initiating the first real tourist industry.

- *Henry Plant* built two hotels, *St. Elmo Inn* and *Port Tampa Inn*, to accommodate his railroad passengers. *Port Tampa City* was built at the end of his rail line. The large *Port Tampa Inn* was constructed in the bay on stilts. Both hotels are long gone, and the town of *Port Tampa* was annexed into *Tampa* in 1961.

• In 1891, *Henry B. Plant* built a lavish 500-room, quarter-mile long luxury resort hotel called the *Tampa Bay Hotel* among 150 acres of manicured gardens along the banks of the *Hillsborough River*. The eclectic structure cost $2.5 million to build, a huge sum in those days. Plant filled his expensive playground with exotic art collectables from around the world and installed electric lights and the first elevator in *Florida*.

Old Tampa Bay Hotel

• The *Tampa Bay Hotel* did great business in the late 1800s, especially during the *Spanish-American War*. But with Plant's death in 1899, the hotel's fortunes began to fade. The city of *Tampa* purchased the resort in 1905 and used it for different community events, including the first state fair. It was closed in 1930, and re-opened in 1933 as the *University of Tampa*.

• *Florida* does not have one great metropolitan area as a focal point; *Tampa Bay* is only one, along with *Miami, Orlando* of course, and the *Jacksonville* area. It is over 700 miles to drive from *Key West* to *Pensacola* – that will literally take you across three or four states in a normal travel route.

• The *Second Seminole War* began in December 1835, when troops led by Maj. Francis L. Dade were ambushed on their way from *Fort Brooke* (Tampa) to *Fort King* (Ocala) in a rout called the *Dade Massacre*. After nearly 7 years of vicious fighting, The war ended and the *Seminoles* were forced from *Tampa Bay*.

• *Florida* was under colonial rule by *Spain* and *Great Britain* before becoming a U.S. territory, and later (1845) a U.S. state.

• When glaciation locked up the world's water, starting nearly 3 million years ago, the sea level dropped precipitously to 330 feet lower than present levels. As a result, the *Florida* peninsula emerged, with a land area about twice what it is today.

• On March 3, 1845, *Florida* became the 27th state of the *United States of America*. The first governor for the state of *Florida* was William Dunn Moseley, a descendant of English immigrants who settled in America in 1649.

• Until the 1900s *Florida* was the least populated state in the *South*, and even after *Florida* became the most populated Southern state, it was not considered "a true Southern state" with an economy and history unlike the rest of the *South*.

• In 1834 *Augustus Steele* convinced his *Tallahassee* friends to establish 8,580 square miles of West Coast wilderness to be declared *Hillsborough County*, with *Tampa* named as a county capital even though there was no separate village.

• The "Village of Tampa" settlement was incorporated in 1849 with 185 inhabitants, excluding military personnel who were stationed at *Fort Brooke*. The city's first official census in 1850 listed *Tampa-Fort Brooke* as having 974 residents. *Tampa* was re-incorporated as a town on December 15, 1855, and *Judge Joseph B. Lancaster* became the first Mayor in 1856.

• *Florida* seceded from the *United States* January 10, 1861 and joined in the formation of the *Confederate States of America*. *Fort Brooke* was manned by Confederate troops and martial law was declared in *Tampa* in January 1862. The city government ceased to operate for the duration of the *Civil War*.

• The *Belleview Hotel* was opened in 1897 by *Henry B. Plant* as a resort destination on his *Orange Belt Railway* serving the west coast of Florida. He built a spur rail to the hotel for the seasonal guests. The *Atlantic Coast Line Railroad*, which absorbed the *Plant System* lines in 1902, continued to operate the *Pinellas Special* train from New York City to a siding on the hotel's property in the 1920s. This rail spur was abandoned after 1946.

Belleview Hotel on the Orange Belt Railway

• The *Pinellas Trail* is built on the remnants of the *Orange Belt Railway*. The railway ran from *St. Petersburg* through *Pinellas* to *Tarpon Springs* where it veered east and continued to *Sanford*.

• The *Largo* area was once called *Armour* and had its own station on the *Orange Belt Railroad*. The name came from an investor of the *Orange Belt*, C.H. Armour of Philadelphia, who was a brother of the famous meat packer of Chicago.

• The *Orange Belt Railway* was at first a real estate promotion, using mule power and wood rails from *Longwood to Myrtle Lake*. A Russian immigrant, *Petrovitch A. Demensheff*, known as *Demens*, partnered with New York investors to create a 152 mile long mainline between *Sanford* and *St. Petersburg*.

• *Florida* became a major hub for the United States Armed Forces. *Naval Air Station Pensacola* was originally established as a naval station in 1826 and became the first American naval aviation facility in 1917.

• *Tampa International Airport* had its beginnings at *Drew Field*. In the 1920s, a dreary damp marshy land with stretches of sand covered over with a sparse growth of palmetto scrub was purchased from *John H. Drew* by the city as an air field. The Federal government turned it into a military base in 1941. It became the site of Tampa's municipal airport in 1946 and in 1950, *Tampa International Airport*. Then in 1952, a brand new terminal was built on the south side of the east-west runway.

• In 2011, *CNNGo* (on CNN Travel Network) listed *Tampa International Airport* as one of the 10 best airports. *TIA* handled 16,820,859 passengers in 2012, making it the 31st busiest airport in North America by passenger movements.

• On January 1, 1914, *Percival Fansler's* "St. Petersburg-Tampa Airboat Line" became the world's first scheduled passenger airline service, carrying passengers between the yacht basin in *St. Pete* and the *Hillsborough River* in downtown *Tampa*. The airline was in operation for four months.

• A trip between *Tampa* and *St. Pete* would take two hours by steamship in 1913, or anywhere from 4 to 12 hours by rail. The trip by automobile was an adventurous 20 hours around the bay on unpaved roads.

• The *Ocklawaha* and the *Concord Stagecoach Lines* carried passengers & freight between *Brooksville* and *Tampa* from the 1850s to around 1907. The Concord line cut through the center of now *Pasco County*. One rest stop at *Ehren* near the well field was known as "26 Mile House" in the 1880s.

• In 1850 the entire area between *Hillsborough County* and *Levy County* was named *Benton County*, for U.S. Sen. *Thomas Hart Benton*. When he began to speak against slavery, the *Florida Legislature* changed the county name to *Hernando*.

• *Fort Brooke*, the seed from which *Tampa* had germinated, had served its purpose and was decommissioned in 1883. All traces of the fort are gone except for two cannons displayed on the nearby *University of Tampa* campus.

• *Florida* was originally *Orange Island*, a low-relief island sitting atop the carbonate *Florida Platform*. The first land animals entered the island area that is now *Florida* approximately 24.8 million years ago.

Butterfly McQueen

• Originally a dancer, 28-year-old *Thelma "Butterfly" McQueen* made her debut appearance as an actress in the role of Prissy, Scarlett O'Hara's maid in the 1939 film *Gone with the Wind*. She was born in Tampa, and planned to become a nurse until her teacher suggested that she try acting. *"Butterfly"* became her nickname as a tribute to her constantly moving hands - during her performance of the *Butterfly Ballet* in *A Midsummer Night's Dream*. She had always hated her birth name, and legally changed her name to Butterfly McQueen. She never married or had children. Her film credits run continuously from 1939 until 1989.

• Due to the low latitude of the state, it was chosen in 1949 as a test site for the country's nascent missile program. *Patrick Air Force Base* and the *Cape Canaveral* launch site began to take shape as the 1950s progressed.

• In 1950, *Florida* was ranked twentieth among the states in population; 50 years later it was ranked number four. Due to low tax rates and warm climate, *Florida* became the destination for many retirees from the Northeast, Midwest and Canada.

• Conditions in the city of *Tampa* deteriorated to the point that residents voted to dis-incorporate the city in 1869. Following the *Civil War*, disease, and disinterest had put the city into a slow downward spiral.

• *Tampa* was re-incorporated in 1872. The see-saw population fell from approximately 885 in 1861 to 796 in 1870 and there were only 720 residents listed in the 1880 census.

• *Disney* selected *Orlando* over several other sites for an updated version of their *Disneyland* park in California. In 1971, the *Magic Kingdom*, the first component of the resort, opened and became Florida's best known attraction, attended by tens of millions of visitors a year, spinning off many other attractions.

• Following the defeat of the *Confederacy* to end the *Civil War*, a state convention was held in 1865 to rewrite the constitution of *Florida*. After meeting the requirements of Reconstruction, including ratifying amendments to the *U.S. Constitution*, *Florida* was re-admitted to the United States on July 25, 1868.

• *Florida College* is a small, regionally accredited, coeducational Christian college located eight miles northeast of *Tampa*. It was founded as a junior college in 1946, and is located in the heart of *Temple Terrace*, astride the banks of the *Hillsborough River*.

• Two of the oldest buildings in *Temple Terrace* are an integral part of the *Florida College* campus; *Sutton Hall*, circa 1922, the original clubhouse for the *Temple Terrace Golf & Country Club*, and the *Student Center* was originally the *Club Morocco Nightclub and Casino*, circa 1926.

• *Club Morocco,* the hottest nightclub on the west coast of *Florida* in the 1920s, along with several other buildings in the city, were designed by noted *Tampa* architect *M. Leo Elliott.*

• Turbine-powered flights into *Tampa* began in 1959 on *Eastern Air Lines'* Lockheed L-188 Electra; in 1960 *National, Eastern and Delta Air Lines* began jet flights with the Douglas DC-8 (*Delta* was first, with a Chicago nonstop). Weekly flights to *Mexico City* began in 1961 on *Pan American*.

• The *Gasparilla Pirate Festival* is held in *Tampa* every year in late January or early February, to celebrate the apocryphal legend of *José Gaspar*, a mythical Spanish pirate captain who supposedly operated in Southwest Florida. It began in 1904, when a civic association of local businessmen first dubbed themselves *Ye Mystic Krewe of Gasparilla*, and then staged an "invasion" of the city followed by a parade and city-wide party.

• The *Bonnie Blue Flag*, a single white star on a blue field, was the flag of the short-lived *Republic of West Florida*. Decades later, during the *Civil War*, it became an unofficial banner of the *Confederacy*, inspiring the song *"The Bonnie Blue Flag,"* which was often sung by Southern troops. The flag was created by *Melissa Johnson*, wife of *Major Isaac Johnson*, commander of the *West Florida Dragoons*. On September 11, 1810, settlers in the *Spanish* territory of *West Florida* revolted against the *Spanish* government and proclaimed an independent republic. The *Bonnie Blue Flag* was raised at the *Spanish* fort in *Baton Rouge* on September 23, 1810. On December 6, 1810, *West Florida* was annexed by the *United States* and the republic ceased to exist as an independent entity, after a life of 74 days.

• *Jessica Ann Sierra* a singer from *Tampa*, and a contestant on the fourth season of *American Idol* in 2005, released her single recording *Enough* in October 2010.

• The two largest freshwater lakes in *Pinellas County*, *Lake Tarpon* (accessible through Chestnut and Anderson parks) and *Lake Seminole* (accessible through Lake Seminole Park), are popular for water skiing, jet-skiing, and sailing, as well as for fishing and kayaking.

• Agriculture was the single most important industry in *Pinellas County* until the early 20th century, with much of the best land devoted to citrus production and cattle ranching.

• In 1885 the *American Medical Society* declared the Pinellas peninsula the "healthiest spot on earth", which helped spur the growth of the tourist industry.

• As Florida's 6th and the nation's 53rd most populous county, Pinellas has a population greater than that of the individual states of Wyoming, Montana, Delaware, South Dakota, Alaska, North Dakota, and Vermont, as well as the District of Columbia.

• With a population density (as of the 2010 Census) of 3,300/sq. mile, *Pinellas County* is by far the most densely populated county in the state, more than double that of *Broward County*, the next most densely populated, and almost ten times the state average state density of 350/sq. mi. The median age was 46.3 years. Females made up 52% of the population.

• *Pinellas County* gained some national attention as the home of the *Mystery Monkey of Tampa Bay*, a non-native, feral rhesus macaque that was on the loose for approximately three years in the south of the county. No one is sure where the monkey came from. A *Facebook* page set up for the monkey had over 84,000 likes (October 2012). The monkey was the subject of a sketch on the March 11, 2010 episode of the *Colbert Report*. Efforts to capture the monkey were reignited after it reportedly bit a woman living near where it had taken up residence, and the monkey was captured in late October 2012 and sent to live at *Dade City's Wild Things*, a 22-acre zoo north of *Tampa*.

• *Babe Ruth* was once a guest of *The Tampa Bay Hotel* during its latter days, and signed his first baseball contract in the Grand Dining Room. According to local legend, he hit his longest home run ever at the *old Tampa Fairgrounds* stadium located on the hotel grounds.

• *Evelyn Brent*, an American film and stage actress, born *Mary Elizabeth Riggs* in *Tampa*, appeared in 70 silent films from 1915 to 1928 before making a successful transition into the talkies in 1928. After performing in more than 120 films, she retired from acting in 1950. However, she returned to acting in television's *Wagon Train* in 1960. Evelyn was honored with a star on the *Hollywood Walk of Fame* for her majestic contribution to the motion picture industry.

Evelyn Brent

• In 1885, the *Tampa Board of Trade* helped broker a deal with *Vicente Martinez Ybor* to move his cigar manufacturing to *Tampa* from *Key West*. Close proximity to Cuba made imports of tobacco easy by sea, and Plant's railroad made shipment of finished cigars to the rest of the U.S. market easy by land.

• Before 1900 Ybor's success quickly established *Tampa* as a major cigar production center. The settlement was dubbed *Ybor City,* and several other cigar factories soon moved in.

• *Sarasota County* (Sarasota) was formed in 1921 from *Manatee County*. The reason for the name is not documented. It is believed it is for either a Calusa word that means *"point of rocks"* or *"place of the dance,"* or possibly for *Sara de Soto*, the daughter of famed area explorer *Hernando de Soto*.

• Although *Sarasota County* was created in 1921, the area is rich in history and heritage, and the pride of the community is reflected in the preservation of the past.

• The beaches of *Sarasota County* are world famous, but the sophistication of the area surprises newcomers to the region. The county's high per capita income supports a wide variety of recreational activities and arts organizations including theater, ballet, opera and international film festivals usually found only in larger urban areas. However, a low cost of living makes the Sarasota lifestyle very affordable, and it continually ranks among the nation's 15 most livable communities.

• When *Sarasota County* was formed in 1921, the population was 4,439. Three-fourths lived in the City of Sarasota or nearby. Venice totaled 200. In 1996 the population of *Sarasota County* had reached more than 300,000 and Venice itself had nearly quadrupled the total countywide population of 1921.

• *Lee County* (Fort Myers) was formed in 1887, some 20 years after the Civil War, and named for Confederate general *Robert E. Lee*. It is the only county in Florida that is named for a soldier of the Civil War - either side.

• *Union County* (Lake Butler) was formed in 1921 from Bradford County. It was named to pay tribute to all the Northern forces in the American *Civil War*.

Gen. Robert E. Lee

• The 35 miles of beaches and dunes which make up *Pinellas County's* 11 barrier islands provide habitat for coastal species, serve as critical storm protection for the inland communities, and form the basis of the area's thriving tourism industry. The islands are dynamic, with wave action building some islands further up, eroding others, and forming entirely new islands over time.

• Though hurricanes are infrequent in the *Tampa Bay* area, they have had a major impact on the barrier islands along the west coast of *Pinellas County*. The Hurricane of 1848 formed *John's Pass* between *Madeira Beach* and *Treasure Island*, a hurricane in 1921 created *Hurricane Pass* and cleaved *Hog Island* into *Honeymoon* and *Caladesi Islands*, and 1985's Hurricane Elena sealed *Dunedin Pass* to join *Caladesi* with *Clearwater Beach*.

• *Pinellas County* forms a peninsula bounded on the west by the *Gulf of Mexico* and on the south and east by *Tampa Bay*, to form Florida's second-smallest county after *Union County*. The entire peninsula is 38 miles long and 15 miles wide at its broadest point, but includes 587 miles of coastline.

• Both *Delta Air Lines and US Airways* closed their maintenance bases at *Tampa International* following the terror attacks on September 11, 2001 and the airline struggles that ensued.

17

• Although her active career in television and movies actually started in 2001, *Brittany Snow*, who was born and grew up in *Tampa*, and graduated from *Gaither High School*, headlined her first movie, *Prom Night*, in 2008. Her success in that role launched a flurry of lead roles in movies and TV.

• When the *Florida territory* was acquired from Spain by the U.S. in 1821, President *John Quincy Adams* appointed *Gen. Andrew Jackson* as "military" governor. Jackson served less than a year in that capacity, and later became the U.S. President from Tennessee.

Brittany Snow

• *Dawna Stone*, founder and publisher of *Her Sports* magazine, was hired by *Martha Stewart* on *The Apprentice: Martha Stewart*, which ran during the fall of 2005. A strong advocate of improving women's health and fitness, Dawna was featured on her own popular monthly healthy living television segment on *Good Day Tampa Bay*. She lives in *St. Petersburg*, with her husband, Matt, and their two dogs, Buffett and Valkyrie (Val).

• *Horr's Island*, located on the south side of *Marco Island* in *Collier County,* is one of the oldest known mound burials in the eastern United States, dating back nearly 4,000 years. It was one of the largest known communities permanently occupied during the Archaic period (8000 BC-2000 BC).

18

• The first ship docked at *Port Manatee* in 1970; a deepwater seaport located in the *Gulf of Mexico* at the entrance to *Tampa Bay* in northern *Manatee County*. It is the closest U.S. port to the *Panama Canal;* served by mostly cargo ships, but the *Regal Empress* cruise ship sailed out of the port until the early 2000s.

• The first time *Europeans* explored what is known today as *Hillsborough County* was in the 16th Century. *Spanish* conquistadors, *Panfilo de Narvaez* and *Hernando DeSoto*, came in search of gold. They only found *Tocobagan Indians*.

• There are more than 1,250 golf courses across *Florida*. In fact, *Florida* has more golf courses than any other U.S. state.

• *Gulf Coast Limited* made its first stop at the *St. Petersburg Atlantic Coast Line* depot Dec. 1, 1927. The train originated in Jacksonville but also carried through the Pullman sleeper cars and coaches from all connecting trains traveling down the east coast. It crossed from the north-east tip of *Florida* to the southwest; *St. Pete* was the "end of the line."

• During the first few decades of the 20th century, the cigar making industry was the backbone of the *Tampa* economy. In the peak year of 1929, more than 500,000,000 cigars were hand rolled in *Ybor City* and *West Tampa*.

• *Mary Hatcher* is a singer and actress from *Tampa*, whose screen career spanned the years from 1946 to 1951. In 1947 she landed the title role in Paramount's all-star revue *Variety Girl*. The film provided cameo performances by practically every player the studio had under contract, including *Bing Crosby,*

Gary Cooper, Bob Hope, & *Burt Lancaster*. *Hatcher* returned to *Tampa* for a gala opening of the film at the *Tampa Theatre*. Large crowds turned out to honor their home-town movie star, and Tampa mayor *Curtis Hixon* presented *Mary* with a golden key to the city.

Mary Hatcher

• *Ponce de Leon* was not searching for a *Fountain of Youth*, a popular myth of the times; he was ousted from *Puerto Rico*, the colony he started, and set out to find a huge island he heard about from Cuban fishermen. He found what he was looking for, and became the first person to verify that *Florida* was not an island, but a peninsula attached to the same mainland of North America as Mexico.

• On June 2, 1887, Florida Governor *E. A. Perry* signed into law a unique and unusual measure passed by the Legislature that called for the division of *Hernando County* into three parts to create *Citrus, Pasco*, and *Hernando counties*.

20

• *William Pope Duval* was the first civilian governor of Florida Territory, serving from April 17, 1822 until April 24, 1834. In 1821, when Florida became a U.S. Territory, Duval, a former U.S. Congressman from Kentucky, was named U. S. Judge for the East Florida district.

• On April 17, 1822, President *James Monroe* appointed Duval as the first non-military governor of the territory, succeeding Gen. *Andrew Jackson*. He was reappointed by President *John Quincy Adams* and President *Andrew Jackson*.

• During his twelve year administration, *Governor William Duval* relocated the territory's capital to Tallahassee.

•The *Coliseum* in *St. Petersburg* is the finest ballroom in the South. It opens its oak dance floor for everything from dancing to corporate functions. The historic Coliseum was built in 1924, and purchased by the *City of St. Petersburg* in 1989. The *Coliseum* has undergone extensive renovations, making it one of the *Tampa Bay* area's most unique multi-use facilities. The *Coliseum* is located in the *St. Petersburg* historic district.

• The *Travel Channel* rated the *Sunshine Skyway Bridge* as number 3 in their list of the "Top 10 Bridges" in the World.

• The southbound span of the original *Sunshine Skyway Bridge* opened in 1971, and was destroyed at 7:30 a.m. on May 9, 1980, when the freighter *MV Summit Venture* collided with a support pier during a storm. More than 1200 feet of the bridge plummeted into Tampa Bay, causing ten cars and a Greyhound bus to fall 150 feet into the water. Thirty-five people were killed, leaving only one survivor.

• In 2012, the *U.S. Postal Service* recognized the twenty-fifth anniversary of *Florida's Sunshine Skyway Bridge* by issuing the $5.15 *Sunshine Skyway Bridge Priority Mail* stamp. In the stamp artwork, the bridge rises from the vivid blue water of *Tampa Bay*, and is silhouetted against an orange sky. Tiny vehicles on the road reveal the massive scale of this miraculous engineering feat.

• The *Sunshine Skyway Bridge* carries more than 50,000 cars a day over the entrance to *Tampa Bay*. The north end is in *St. Petersburg* (Pinellas County), and the south end is in *Terra Ceia* (Manatee County). The bridge was opened to traffic on April 20, 1987. It is 5.5 miles long, and the main span is 1,200 feet long, with a clearance of 193 feet above the water; for vessels entering the port of Tampa.

• *Sunshine Skyway Bridge*, at 4.1 miles from shore to shore, is the largest cable suspension bridge in the Western Hemisphere. It actually rises 19 stories above *Tampa Bay* at midpoint.

• In 2005, an act of *Florida Legislature* officially named the current bridge the *Bob Graham Sunshine Skyway Bridge*, after the Governor of Florida and then U.S. Senator who presided over its design and most of its construction.

• In late June 2012 *Tropical Storm Debby* forced *Sunshine Skyway* bridge's longest closure. More than 48 hours of 40 mph sustained winds left the bridge closed for the longest time since it opened in 1987. The longest closure previously was in 2001, during *Tropical Storm Gabrielle*. That "long-term" closure lasted slightly more than eight hours.

• *The Battle of Olustee* or *Battle of Ocean Pond* was fought in *Baker County, Florida* on February 20, 1864, during the American *Civil War*. It was the largest battle fought in *Florida* during the war.

• Following *Abraham Lincoln's* election as President in 1860, *Florida* joined other Southern states in seceding from the Union, and became one of the founding members of the *Confederate States of America*.

• During the *Civil War*, Union forces operated a blockade around the entire state, and occupied major ports such as *Jacksonville, Cedar Key, Pensacola,* and *Key West*. Though numerous deadly skirmishes occurred in *Florida*, the only major *Civil War* battle was the *Battle of Olustee* near *Lake City*.

• Located at the extreme southern tip of the *Confederacy* during the *Civil War*, *Florida* was so far from the major battlefields that it had its own *Civil War*. The coastline was too large to protect, but fast-moving *Florida* cavalry kept the *Union* from destroying all the needed salt fields and cattle centers.

• *Tallahassee* was the only Southern capital east of the Mississippi that never fell to the *Union*; but *Florida* units (fighting far from home) experienced some of the highest casualty rates of the war.

•*Blondie* has several ties to *Tampa Bay. Murat Bernard Young* (1901-1973), better known as *Chic Young*, created the popular, long-running comic strip *Blondie*, which had a daily readership of 52 million. Young moved to Florida in the 1960s where he stated "We reside on a little island off the west coast of Florida, where the porpoises and pelicans entertain me while I work on the strip." He continued to draw *Blondie* at his home in *St. Petersburg*, until his death in 1973 at age 72.

Chic Young

• Upon the death of *Chic Young*, his son, *Dean Wayne Young*, inherited the *Blondie* franchise, and continued to create the strip from his home in *St. Pete*. The *Blondie* comic strip was appearing in 1,600 newspapers worldwide.

• *John Marshall* began assisting on *Blondie* in 2002 and became head artist in May 2005. Marshall began his cartooning career at the age of 14, and in 1976 he graduated from *Ringling School of Art* in *Sarasota* with honors. He worked as art director at an ad agency in New York until 1980, when he began a career as freelance artist that lasted over 20 years.

25

• *Rondo K. Hatton* grew up in *Tampa*, where family members owned a business. *Acromegaly*, a disorder of the pituitary gland, distorted the shape of Hatton's head, face, and extremities in a gradual but consistent process. Hatton, who had been voted the handsomest boy in his class at *Hillsborough High School*, eventually became severely disfigured by the disease. Hatton worked as a reporter with *The Tampa Tribune*, and while covering the filming of *Hell Harbor* (1930), Director Henry King noticed him and hired him for a small role in the film. *Universal Studios* then attempted to exploit Hatton's unusual features to promote him as a horror star.

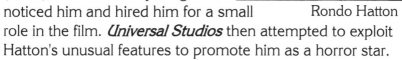

Rondo Hatton

• *Rondo Hatton* of *Tampa* played the part of the *Hoxton Creeper* in the 1944 *Sherlock Holmes* film, *The Pearl of Death*, and several more films playing the same character. Hatton died of a heart attack (a result of his Acromegaly) in 1946, and was returned to *Tampa* for burial in *American Legion Cemetery*.

Robin Zander

• In 2007, when *Cheap Trick* (referred to as the "American Beatles"), honored the 40th anniversary of the Beatles' *Sgt. Pepper's Lonely Hearts Club Band*, they staged concerts in New York, L.A. and *Clearwater*. That's because *Robin Zander*, the singer for the power-pop legends, calls *Safety Harbor* home. It was supposedly too difficult to be re-created onstage. But no one told *Cheap Trick*; they performed it live at *Ruth Eckerd Hall* in 2008.

• Tampa's first zoo was a small collection of exotic animals in *Plant Park* on the grounds of the *University of Tampa* across the *Hillsborough River* from downtown.

• Actress *Lauren Hutton* (Mary Laurence Hutton) graduated from *Chamberlain High School* in *Tampa*, in 1961, and was among the first students to attend the *University of South Florida* in 1960. Hutton was a *Playboy Bunny* at age 20, and made her film debut in the *Paper Lion* (1968). The slight gap in her teeth gave Hutton a distinctive on-camera persona, and she was known as "the fresh American face of fashion." In 1974, she signed a million-dollar contract as the *face of Revlon cosmetics*.

Lauren Hutton

• *West Tampa* is one of the oldest neighborhoods within the city limits of *Tampa*. It was an independently incorporated city from 1895 until 1925, when it was officially annexed by *Tampa*.

• Located west of the *Hillsborough River* about one mile from downtown, *West Tampa* has consistently been home to one of the highest concentration of Latinos in the city.

• *Tampa Bay* native *Mardy Fish* married *Stacey Gardner*, a *"Briefcase Model"* on NBC's *Deal or No Deal*, in 2008. Fish attended *Vero Beach High School* for three years and his senior year at *Boca Prep in Boca Raton.* In April 2011, he was America's No. 1 ATP tennis pro.

• *Florida's* first theme parks emerged in the 1930s and included *Cypress Gardens* (1936) near *Winter Haven* and *Marineland* (1938) near *St. Augustine.*

• Due to the large amount of water locked up in glaciers during the Wisconsin glaciation, the sea level was more than 300 feet lower than present levels. The *Florida* peninsula had a land area about twice what it is today.

• The *Seminole Indians* developed as a distinct tribe in *Florida* during the 18th century. They are an offshoot of the *Creek* people who commonly absorbed other groups,

• When the *Spanish* attempted to settle in *Florida* in the early 1500s, there were an estimated 150,000 inhabitants who spoke in dialects of the *Timucua* language. However, the *Timucua* were groups who did not share a common culture.

• *Andrew Jackson* formally took control of *Florida* from the *Spanish* authorities on July 17, 1821 at Pensacola. He became the first military *Governor of Florida* as an organized territory of the U. S. on March 30, 1822. In 1845 *Florida* became a state.

• *University of South Florida Sarasota-Manatee* was established in 1975, and shared a campus with the *New College of Florida* until a new campus was built for *USF Sarasota Manatee*. The new campus opened on August 28, 2006.

• The *University of Tampa* is a private, co-educational university in Downtown Tampa. In 2006, the University celebrated its 75th anniversary. UT offers over 100 undergraduate degree options, along with master's degree programs.

• The first three historic sites in *Sarasota County* to be placed on the *National Register of Historic Places* are prehistoric. They are *Historic Spanish Point, Little Salt Springs and Warm Mineral Springs*. Since 1980, a total of 52 sites have been added, along with six historic districts.

• *Tampa International Airport*, widely praised for its attractive architecture, is known as the world's friendliest airport.

• The 1952 passenger terminal at *Tampa* was built for three airlines. It was swamped after the *Civil Aeronautics Board* granted *Capital, Delta, Northeast, Northwest and Trans World Airlines* authority to fly to *Tampa* in the late 1950s. An annex was built east of the terminal for the new carriers.

28

• The *Don CeSar Hotel*, in all it's pink glory, is listed on the *National Register of Historic Places*.

• The *Don CeSar* is the culmination of Thomas Rowe's vision of a castle-like hotel to parallel the Royal Hawaiian Hotel on Waikiki Beach. In the mid 1920s, Rowe hired Henry Dupont to design the hotel. The Mediterranean/Moorish design was originally intended to be a six-story, 110 room hotel built on a $450,000 budget, the project evolved into a 220 room $1.25 million hotel - 300 percent over budget.

• In 1926 *St. Petersburg* became a regular get away for *Al Capone*. Although he was a frequent guest at the *Don Cesar Beach Resort*, it is also rumored that Capone owned a home in *Shore Acres* that was used by his elderly mother.

• *Al Capone's* favorite *Florida* hangout was *Derby Lanes* (known at that time as the *St Petersburg Kennel Club*).

• Rowe's "Pink Lady" in *St. Petersburg* opened Jan. 16, 1928, and quickly became a favorite romping ground for the rich and famous of the *Jazz Age* including *F. Scott Fitzgerald, Clarence Darrow, Al Capone, Lou Gehrig,* and *Franklin D. Roosevelt*. The *Pink Palace* continued to attract the rich and famous during the *Great Depression*, thanks to a deal with *New York Yankees* owner *Jacob Ruppert* to house his team during spring training.

• *Mark Consuelos* (better known as *Mr. Kelly Ripa*) attended *Bloomingdale High* in *Valrico* and graduated from the *University of South Florida*. Consuelos was born to a Mexican father and

an Italian mother. He does not speak Spanish, he does speak Italian. He met *Kelly Ripa*, his co-star on *All My Children*, in 1995. They married in 1996. The two continued to tape episodes of *All My Children* until 2002.

• *Sandra W. Freedman* was the first female mayor of *Tampa*. She served on the City Council from 1974 and was Council Chair from 1983 -1986. She completed the term of *Bob Martinez* who resigned to run for Governor of Florida. After completing Martinez's term, Sandra Freedman was twice elected *Mayor of Tampa,* serving from 1987 until 1995.

Mark & Kelly

• *Odessa* is a community located in both *Hillsborough County*, and *Pasco County*. The population was 3,173 at the 2000 census, with about half in each county. Originally, there was a large sawmill in the area, employing many people.

• *Christopher Keith Irvine*, a *Tampa* resident, who is known professionally as *Chris Jericho*, a professional wrestler, actor, musician, author and businessman, competed in *Dancing With The Stars* in 2011. He survived until the 6th week. *Jericho*, is a six-time world champion, and record nine-time Intercontinental Champion. As a musician, he is best known as lead vocalist for the heavy metal band *Fozzy*, which has released four albums.

• Award winning actor *John Travolta* is a certified private pilot and owns five aircraft, including an ex-Qantas Boeing 707 airliner. The plane bears the name *Jett Clipper Ella* after his children. Travolta serves as a goodwill ambassador for the *Qantas* airline. His $4.9 million estate in *Ocala* is situated on *Greystone Airport* with its own runway and taxiway right to his front door. Travolta & actress *Kelly Preston* were married in 1991.

• During the final season of her talk show in 2010, *Oprah Winfrey* took her entire studio audience on an all expenses-paid 8-day trip to Australia, with *John Travolta* serving as pilot for the trip. He also helped plan the entire trip.

• Celebrity pilot *John Travolta*, with his wife *Kelly Preston*, flew his own Boeing 707 to *Haiti*, to deliver six tons of rations and medical supplies, along with doctors and ministers from the *Church of Scientology*, after the devastating earthquake in 2012 that left as many as 200,000 people dead and some 2 million in need of aid. *Travolta* had previously used his aircraft to help out during the floods that followed *Hurricane Katrina* in 2005.

• *Weeki Wachee Spring* is the headwaters of the beautiful *Weeki Wachee River*. The spring has been explored to depths of 150 feet, but divers have not located the bottom of this miraculous body of water which pushes 170 million gallons of 99.8 percent pure water to the surface every 24 hours.

• "Weekiwachee" is a *Seminole Indian* word meaning "little spring" and/or "winding river." Newton Perry, an ex-Navy frogman, purchased the land in 1946. He built the underwater theater, and presented the first live, underwater mermaid show.

• *American Broadcasting Company* (ABC) bought *Weeki Wachee Spring* in 1959 and launched a $3 million, 20 year expansion and improvement program. The 200-acre family entertainment park includes *Buccaneer Bay* water park, animal shows, river cruise boat rides and manatee watching. The park is now an official *Florida State Park* .

• *Weeki Wachee* is a city located in *Hernando County*, with a total population of 12 according to the U. S. Census Bureau. The 12,000-acre *Weekiwachee Preserve* and *Weeki Wachee Springs* park are located within the area. The *Weeki Wachee Gardens* and *Spring Hill* residential communities are nearby.

• From May 22 until August 30, 2007, the discharge level at *Weeki Wachee* spring dropped to a level that allowed for cave divers to gain effective entry into the spring's cave system. The *Karst Underwater Research* team explored approximately 6,700 feet in multiple passages to a maximum depth of 407 feet.

• *Citrus County* is known as "The Little Giant" as inscribed on the official county seal. *Citrus County* is also in the geographic center of *Florida*. *Citrus County* was named for the county's citrus trees; but citrus production in the area declined drastically after the "Big Freeze" of 1894-1895.

• *Citrus County* is currently the only place in the United States where one can legally swim with the *West Indian Manatee*.

• The *Manatee*, an endangered species makes its winter home in the spring-fed rivers of *Citrus County*. According to the U.S. Fish & Wildlife Services, as many as 400 of these unique creatures can be found in Citrus County at one time.

• *Baughman Center* located along *Lake Alice* on the *University of Florida* campus, was initiated by *Dr. George Baughman,* a UF alumnus, and the first president of *New College of Florida* in *Sarasota*. He and his wife Hazel donated $1 million towards the project, which was completed in 2000. Baughman died in 2004, and a memorial service was held in the chapel at UF.

• *George F. Baughman* was the first president of *New College of Florida*, a vice president of the *University of Florida* as well as of *New York University* and a rear admiral in the *United States Naval Reserve*. Baughman was born in *Tampa*, and educated at the *University of Florida*.

• When *Hernando DeSoto* landed at *Shaw's Point*, near the mouth of *Tampa Bay* in 1539, what is now *Manatee County* was the southern boundary for the *Tocobagan* tribe.

• *Pasco County* was named in honor of *Samuel Pasco*, the President of the *1885 Florida Constitutional Convention*, Speaker of the *Florida House of Representatives*, and two-term U.S. Senator from Florida. He resided near Tallahassee and is never known to have visited the County that bears his name.

• The *Black Hills Passion Play* was a major tourist attraction in *Polk County* from 1953 until 1998. *Josef Meier* performed reenactments of the last days of Jesus Christ as reported in the gospels, with his own English language version. In 1939 he opened a permanent home for his play in the Black Hills of South Dakota. In 1953 an amphitheater in *Lake Wales, Florida*, became the winter home for the show, with Meier continuing to portray Jesus until his retirement after more than fifty years in the role. The show continued in *Lake Wales* until 1998.

• In 1884, sixty Scottish families set up a colony and soon built a golf course. With excellent weather, golf and fishing, the town of *Sarasota* was very quickly in the tourism business.

• In 1842, *Josiah Gates* settled the area that became *Manatee County* in 1855, and two brothers named *Hector* and *Joseph Braden* became the major landowners. The county was named after the sea cow that frequents area waters and the Braden's gave their name to a river and the town of *Bradenton*.

• Because Florida's original natives called the *Pasco County* area home, and since that same area experienced many invasions by Spanish conquistadors, *Pasco County* holds a Native American and Spanish heritage celebration each spring. It is called the *Chasco Fiesta* in honor of the legendary ruler of the *Calusas* people, the gorgeous *Queen Chasco*.

• *Manatee County* is the slowest growing of the three counties that front *Tampa Bay*. In 1970 the population of the county was 97,115, but with people looking for "country atmosphere" at bargain prices, it more than doubled to 215,130 by 1991.

• *Cypress Gardens* near *Winter Haven* was billed as Florida's first commercial tourist theme park. It opened January 2, 1936 as a botanical garden planted by *Dick Pope* and his wife Julie, and soon became one of the biggest attractions in *Florida*. It was known for the magnificent water ski shows, beautiful gardens, and lovely Southern Belles. The arrival of *Walt Disney World* in 1971 and freeways that bypassed *Winter Haven* doomed *Cypress Gardens* to a slow, agonizing death.

• The *Python* at *Busch Gardens* was not only the park's first roller coaster; it was also the first inverting roller coaster in *Florida.* The unique ride was removed from the park in 2006.

• *New Hope Methodist Church* north of *Istachatta* was built of logs with a dirt floor in 1841. It was the earliest church in Hernando County and also served as a school and a fortress from the *Wahoo* Indians.

• The *United States* purchased *Florida* from *Spain* in 1821 in order to end frontier Indians raids and to control escaped slaves fleeing into the area. Spain controlled Florida since the *Treaty of Paris* at the end of the *American Revolution* in 1783. This action made it an official part of the U. S. for the first time.

• The first settlement in the area now known as *Lutz* was a Catholic mission started in the late 1880s by a Luxembourg Catholic priest Francis Xavier Stemper. He purchased acreage on the west side of *Lake Bruing* to start a Catholic colony.

• In 1907 the *Tampa Northern Railroad* was built, connecting *Tampa*, through *Stemper*, towards *Brooksville* and beyond. It effectively put the *Concord Stagecoach Line* out of business.

• *Hurricane Andrew* in August 1992 struck *Homestead*, just south of *Miami* as a Category 5 hurricane, leaving forty people dead, 100,000 homes damaged or destroyed, over a million people without electricity, and damages of $20 - 30 billion.

• *Henry Bradley Plant* was involved with many transportation projects in *Florida*. Eventually he owned the Plant System of railroads which became part of *Atlantic Coast Line Railroad*. *Plant City*, located near *Tampa*, was named after him.

• In preparation for his 1976 *Rolling Thunder Revue* tour, musician *Bob Dylan* spent a month rehearsing at the *Belleview Biltmore* with his troupe. Band members included *Roger McGuinn of The Byrds*, violinist *Scarlet Rivera*, and folk queen *Joan Baez*. They played two shows at the hotel.

• The lumber boom of the late 1800s and early 1900s spawned numerous sawmills in *Tampa Bay*. With much of *Hillsborough* and *Pasco County* covered in pine trees, several mills were here, but the *Ehren Pine Company* in *Pasco County* was the largest. Tram tracks connected the sawmills with surrounding areas.

• *East Florida* was a colony of *Great Britain* from 1763 - 1783 and of *Spain* from 1783 - 1822. *East Florida* was established by the British colonial government with *St. Augustine* as the capital, which had been the capital of *Spanish Florida*.

• Several attempts were made to introduce flamingos to the sanctuary at *Bok Tower Gardens* near *Lake Wales*, which is why early renderings of the tower show flamingos at the reflection pool rather than swans. All efforts were unsuccessful. The flamingos did not survive the winters that were cooler than those of southern Florida where they may be found naturally.

• *Bok Tower Gardens* is a botanical garden and bird sanctuary, located north of *Lake Wales*. It consists of a 250-acre garden, the 205-foot tall Singing Tower with its carillon bells, Pine Ridge Trail, Pinewood Estate, and a visitor center. The tower is built

upon *Iron Mountain*, one of the highest points in *Florida*, sitting at 295 feet above sea level. It is a *National Historic Landmark* that is listed on the *National Register of Historic Places*.

• *Bok Tower Gardens* began in 1921 when *Edward W. Bok*, editor of *Ladies Home Journal,* and his wife, *Mary Louise Curtis Bok*, were spending the winter in Lake Wales and decided to create a bird sanctuary.

• Under construction for over five years, *Bok Tower Gardens* was dedicated by *President Calvin Coolidge* in 1929. *Edward Bok* died in 1930 and was interred at the base of the tower.

• The public is not allowed inside the tower, which contains the *Anton Brees Carillon Library,* the largest carillon library in the world. It was established in 1968 following the death of Anton Brees, the first carillonneur at the Singing Tower. Each year, graduating seniors from *Lake Wales High School* have the opportunity to see the inside of the tower and visit the bell chamber that houses the 60-bell carillon set.

• *Florida Aquarium* in Tampa opened in 1995 as a privately funded entity, and became a public-private partnership when the city of *Tampa* assumed responsibility in 1999.

• Following *Hernando de Soto's* excursion through the region in 1539, the *Spaniards* never again mounted an overland expedition to *Tampa Bay* or the area immediately to the north.

• The *Armed Occupation Act* was signed into law in August of 1842. It encouraged settlers to occupy, clear and use up to 160 acres of remote land, provided it was not within two miles of a military post. It made available 200,000 acres of land in the area that became *Hernando County* the following year.

• In January 1843 a bill was introduced in the *Florida* House to create a new county to be called *Amaxura*, which was the Spanish name for the *Withlacoochee River*. The bill was amended, with the name changed to *Hernando*. The new county was created from parts of *Alachua*, *Hillsborough* and *Mosquito* counties.

• In appreciation of *Sen. Thomas Hart Benton's* role in passing the *Armed Occupation Act*, the settlers petitioned the legislature to change the name of *Hernando County* to *Benton County*. On March 6, 1844, one year after the county was created, the legislature approved changing the name.

• On March 15, 1844 the *Florida* legislature approved an act authorizing *William Pennington* to operate a ferry for ten years on the *Withlacoochee River* at *Fort Clinch*.

• In 1845 a post office was established at *Augusta*, just north of *Brooksville* near *Lake Lindsey* in *Benton County*. *Albert Clark* was named as the postmaster, and when he was murdered in 1860, the post office was discontinued. One of his slaves named *Hamp* was hanged for the crime. It was later learned that Hamp. was paid $200 by Albert Clark's step-son, James Boyd, and Mrs. Clark for taking the life of his master.

• The first railway in *Pinellas County* used narrow-gauge tracks and small steam locomotives. When the railway was taken over by the Plant System in 1895, they converted to standard gauge.

• The north end of *Treasure Island* is marked by *John's Pass,* which is a natural water boundary that separates *Treasure Island* from neighboring *Madeira Beach* to the north.

• A storm surge from the "Great Gale" of 1848 literally punched a hole in the long island that ran along the *Pinellas County* coast to form a water pass. It was discovered by a local fisherman named John, when he returned following the storm. *John's Pass* serves the marine interests as one of the few ways to get from the *Intercoastal Waterway* to the *Gulf of Mexico*.

• Around 1900, *St. Petersburg* experienced a land boom which brought weekend tourists to the beaches. To generate interest in the properties being developed a couple of property owners buried and then "discovered" a couple of wooden chests on the beach, claiming the chests were filled with "treasure." The news spread quickly and people called the area *Treasure Island*.

• The massive *John's Pass* double drawbridge linking *Treasure Island to Madeira Beach*, was completed at a cost of $77 million. The bascule bridge, increases the horizontal clearance for boat traffic from 60 feet to 100 feet, and the vertical clearance over the channel to 27 feet. There are two lanes in each direction, with 8-foot sidewalks.

John's Pass Drawbridge

• When the railroad passed through *Hillsborough County* in 1885, Spanish and Cuban cigar workers moved their families and businesses to *Tampa*. This was the start of one of the largest industries in the area.

• *Tampa* is the only major *Florida* city that is not dependent upon tourism. Therefore in an economic crisis, Tampa is better able to recover quickly and is still the largest city in *Tampa Bay*.

• Phosphate mining was a major industry in the *Citrus County* area until the end of *WWII*. The first newspaper of *Citrus County* was called the *Phosphate Times*.

• From January - March, *Busch Gardens* hosts weekly concerts with popular Big Bands to perform classic or contemporary.

• It was in 1885 that a railroad made its first appearance in *Hernando County.* The old *Brooksville Depot* serves as a proud reminder of the significance played by the railroad. It was not a through line, but it did connect into the mail line at the town of *Croom* on the *Withlocoochee River*. Several rail ventures prospered, but in 1933 all passenger service for *Brooksville* was discontinued by *Atlantic Coast Line*. Today the surviving *CSX* serves three rock mines in the northeastern part of the county.

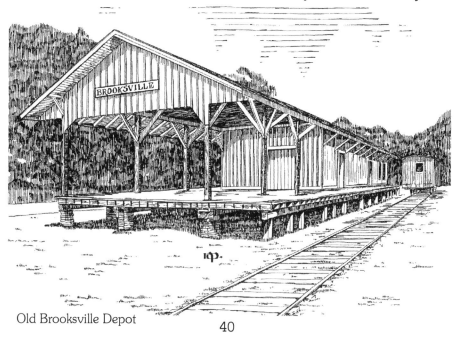

Old Brooksville Depot

• The *Sponge Docks* at *Tarpon Springs* embody the key focus for this unique community. In 1876 the area was known as *Anclote. A. W. Ormond* was standing on the shore of the bayou with his daughter Mary, who saw a tarpon (fish) jump high out of the water. "Look at that tarpon spring!" she exclaimed. Since that

Sponge Docks at Tarpon Springs

time, the town has been called *Tarpon Springs*, and the bayou is known as *Spring Bayou*.

• *Tarpon Springs* was originally incorporated in 1887, with only 46 registered voters. When railroad service to New York was first inaugurated, the vicinity became a very popular winter resort for northern tourists.

• Greek spongers came to *Tarpon Springs* in 1905. They soon developed the world's largest sponge industry, and brought their culture, food, religion and music. By the 1930s there were some 200 boats working the *Gulf of Mexico* from *Appalachicola* to *Key West*, harvesting 3 million dollars worth of sponges annually. A bacterial blight in the 1940s killed the sponges and the industry. *Tarpon Springs* slowly enjoyed a rebirth of the sponge beds to once again become the world's largest sponge exchange.

• The first settlers of what is now known as *Tarpon Springs* were *A. W. Ormond* and his daughter, *Mary*, who came to *Florida* from *Ninety-Six, South Carolina*, in 1876. They built a cabin near *Spring Bayou*. A year later Mary married J. C. Boyer and they started the first family in the vicinity.

41

• *Yellow fever* hit *Tampa* with terrifying regularity throughout the late 1860s and 1870s. Borne by mosquitos from the surrounding swampland, *Tampa* was hit by wave after wave of devastating yellow fever epidemics. The disease was little understood at the time, and many residents simply packed up and left rather than face the mysterious and deadly peril.

• In 1900, *Florida* was largely undiscovered frontier. Most of the Floridians lived within 50 miles of the Georgia border. The population grew from 529,000 in 1900 to 18.3 million in 2009. The population explosion began with the great land boom of the 1920s as *Florida* became a land speculator's paradise.

• The population of *Tampa* in 1840 included seventy-seven whites, ten slaves, and five free blacks. Across the river in what became *Hyde Park* was *Spanishtown Creek*, a small spring with several homes of *Cuban* fishermen and straw basket makers.

• *Henry Flagler* built the *Florida East Coast Railway* from *Jacksonville* to *Key West*. Along the route he provided for his passengers grand accommodations, including *The Ponce de León Hotel in St. Augustine, The Ormond Hotel in Ormond Beach, The Royal Poinciana Hotel and The Breakers Hotel in Palm Beach, and The Royal Palm Hotel in Miami.*

• The antebellum *Gamble Plantation* mansion, built in the 1840s five miles northeast of *Bradenton,* was home to *Major Robert Gamble* and is the headquarters of an extensive sugar plantation; the only surviving plantation house in South Florida.

• The world-class *David A. Straz, Jr. Center for the Performing Arts* in downtown *Tampa*, includes four theatres, a rehearsal hall, a banquet hall and in-house catering.

• Pánfilo de Narváez's expedition explored Florida's west coast in 1528 but was lost at sea upon his attempted seaward escape to Mexico. One of his officers, Álvar Núñez Cabeza de Vaca, survived for nine years, trudging between Florida and Mexico. He returned to Spain and published his observations; which inspired Hernando de Soto's invasion of Florida in 1539.

• *Admiral Farragut Academy* in *St. Petersburg* occupies the former *Jungle Country Club Hotel* and 35 acres of campus on *Boca Ciega Bay*. Shortly after its completion in 1925, this sprawling *Mediterranean Revival* structure was the centerpiece of Walter Fuller's Jungle Subdivision. In 1945 the Hotel was transformed into the *Admiral Farragut Academy*.

Farragut Academy

• Founded in Pine Beach, New Jersey in 1933 under leadership of *Admiral S. S. Robison*, USN, former Superintendent of the *United States Naval Academy* and Brigadier General *Cyrus Radford*, USMC, *Farragut Academy* is America's first preparatory school with Naval training.

• In 1945 *Adm. Farragut Academy* was established in *St. Petersburg*, and at the time when all hotels in the area were being converted from military barracks back to civilian use, the Academy moved into the *Jungle Country Club Hotel*. The school is a *Naval Honor School*, and in 1989 both of the schools became coeducational; and in 1994 the New Jersey school closed. It is named after *Adm. David Glasgow Farragut*, the senior officer of the U. S. Navy during the *Civil War*.

• A strong hurricane in late September 1848 almost completely washed *Tampa*. Every building was damaged or destroyed, including *Fort Brooke*. Many residents stayed to rebuild, but it took desperate lobbying in Washington, DC to persuade the U.S. Army to reconsider a plan to abandon the fort.

• Phosphate, a mineral used to make fertilizers and other products, was discovered in the *Bone Valley* region southeast of *Tampa* in 1883. Soon, the mining and shipping of phosphate became important area industries. The port at *Tampa* still ships millions of tons of phosphate annually, and the area is known as the *"phosphate capital of the world."*

• Scientologist, and *Clearwater* resident *Armando Anthony "Chick" Corea* participated in the birth of the electric jazz fusion movement. A jazz pianist, keyboardist, and composer, Corea took a profound stylistic turn in the early 1970s and started a crossover jazz fusion style that incorporated Latin jazz elements.

• The *Spanish* did not actually establish the first town in *Florida;* the first operational town in *Florida* was *Fort Caroline* started by *French Huguenots* (Protestants) on the *St. Johns River.* The colony was destroyed by the *Spanish* under *Pedro Menendez,* the man who would found *Saint Augustine*, the oldest continuous town in the United States of America.

• Founded in 1565 by Pedro Menéndez de Avilés, *San Agustín* (St. Augustine) is the oldest continuously inhabited European settlement in any U.S. state; third oldest in the Americas, after Santo Domingo, in the Dominican Republic and San Juan, Puerto Rico. Roman Catholic missionaries used *St. Augustine* as a base of operations and established missions throughout what is today the southeastern United States. Missionaries converted 26,000 natives by 1655 according to their records.

• Despite popular belief, *Osceola (symbol for FSU)* was never a *Seminole* chief, yet *Osceola County* was named to "honor the great Seminole fighter." He was not actually a true *Seminole*; his father was most likely an English trader. *Osceola* was, however, the great war organizer of the *Second Seminole War* - the longest, most costly military event in American history.

Brooker Creek

• *Brooker Creek Preserve* represents 8,000 acres of natural *Florida* heritage in the northeast corner of *Pinellas County*. Established by the *Board of Commissioners,* it is managed by *Pinellas County Department of Environmental Management*. The preserve protects a wide diversity of natural communities and provides the last habitat in the region for many species of plants and animals.

• *Brooker Creek Preserve* is supported by public donations through the efforts of *The Friends of Brooker Creek Preserve*, a not-for-profit organization founded as a coalition of citizens, organizations and business groups who share a common interest in the future of *Pinellas County's* last wilderness.

• *Juan Ponce de León* recorded sighting the peninsula for the first time on March 27, 1513, but thought it was an island. He landed on the east coast of the newly discovered land in April, and named the land *La Pascua Florida*, or "Flowery Easter," probably due to the abundant plant life and the fact that he arrived during the *Spanish Easter* feast, *Pascua Florida*.

• Since *Ponce de León* encountered at least one Indian who could speak *Spanish,* he may not have been the first European to reach *Florida*. He returned with equipment and settlers to start a colony in 1521, but they were driven off by repeated attacks from the native population.

• The *Adams-Onís Treaty* was signed between *Spain* and the *United States* on February 22, 1819 and took effect on July 10, 1821. According to the terms of the treaty, the U. S. acquired *Florida* and renounced all claims to *Texas*.

• The 1885 census ranked *Floral City* twice as big as *Miami*, with a population of 300 persons to Miami's 150. In that same census, *Mannfield*, which was to become the county seat of *Citrus County* two years later, had a population of 250 and *Crystal River* had a population of 200. *Tompkinsville*, which later became *Inverness*, had a recorded population of 30.

• *MacKenzie Law Office* in *Brooksville*, was built in 1840 as a home. It is the oldest house in Brooksville, but is best known for its tenure as the law office of *Judge E. S. MacKenzie*. It sits in the heart of downtown, just a half-block from the Courthouse, this old structure will be preserved for its distinguished service to the community as the oldest residence, but will always be a familiar landmark as the *MacKenzie Law Office*.

• *Knocky Parker* was born August 8, 1918 in Palmer, Texas. He moved from *Kentucky* to *Tampa* in 1962, and was a professor at the *University of South Florida* until his death in 1986. He was a world renowned *Dixieland* and *Ragtime Jazz pianist* during the 1940s, 1950s, 1960s, and 1970s.

• A technically proficient pianist, *Knocky Parker* spent most of his career playing pre-swing jazz. Parker picked up much of his early experience playing piano in Western Swing bands based in his native Texas including the *Wanderers* (1935) and the *Light Crust Doughboys* (1937-39). After military service, Parker worked with the *Zutty Singleton-Albert Nicholas Trio*, earned his PhD and became a college professor, teaching English at *Kentucky Wesleyan College* and *Univ. of South Florida*.

Knocky Parker

• *Knocky Parker* performed and recorded fairly regularly throughout his career, working with *Doc Evans*, *Omer Simeon*, *Tony Parenti* and many others including as a piano soloist. He recorded for Texstar (1949), Paradox, GHB, London, many sessions for Audiophile (including a pioneering project from 1960 to record every Scott Joplin rag), Jazzology and Euphonic.

• With the Treaty of Paris in 1763, *Spain* relinquished all claims & rights and transferred *Florida* to the *British Empire.*

• In 1767, the *British* moved the northern boundary of *Florida* to a line extending from the mouth of the *Yazoo River* east to the *Chattahoochee River,* consisting of the lower third of the present states of Mississippi and Alabama. During this time, *Creek* Indians migrated into Florida to form the *Seminole* tribe.

• On June 2, 1887, *Gov. E. A. Perry* signed into law a measure passed by the Legislature to slice *Hernando County* into three parts to create *Citrus, Pasco,* and *Hernando Counties*. The town of *Mannfield* was named as the temporary seat of *Citrus*. For the next 3 years many elections were held, but no location received a majority vote. Finally, in 1891, the voters approved *Inverness*. The votes were 267 for *Inverness*, 258 for *Lecanto*, and one vote for *Gulf Junction*, now a "Ghost town."

• Founded in 1956, USF the *University of South Florida* is the eighth largest university in the nation and the third largest in the state of *Florida*, with a total enrollment of 47,122 students in 2009. *USF* has an autonomous campus in *St. Petersburg*, and branch centers in *Sarasota* and *Lakeland*.

• To ensure the stability of the *Don CeSar Hotel* built on the shifting sand of *St. Pete Beach* and avoid the high cost of sinking so many pilings, contractor *Carlton Beard* devised a floating concrete pad and pyramid footings. To this day there is no sign of evident settling of the hotel.

• *Stephen King*, the award winning author of contemporary horror, suspense and fantasy fiction, maintains three different homes, one in Bangor, one in Lovell, Maine, and a waterfront mansion located off the *Gulf of Mexico*, in *Sarasota, Florida*. His books have sold more than 350 million copies and have been adapted into a feature films, TV movies and comic books.

• One of the first *Spanish* explorers to land in North America, *Hernando de Soto* came ashore with his men and 200 horses near what is now *Bradenton* in 1539; a national park now commemorates De Soto's expedition. During tourist season, from December to April, park staff and volunteers dress in period costumes and demonstrate the use of 16th-century weapons, as well as lifestyles of European explorers.

• *Pam Iorio* was sworn in as *Mayor of Tampa* in 2003; the second woman to hold the office. Iorio earned her bachelor degree from *American University* and her masters at the *University of South Florida*, where her father *John Iorio*, an Italian immigrant, was a professor.

• *Kumba*, meaning *roar* in *Swahili*, is one of the two most popular rides at *Busch Gardens Tampa Bay*. It is a 143-foot steel sit-down roller coaster with seven inversions. First built in 1993 by *Bolliger & Mabillard*, it was repainted in 2010.

• *Busch Gardens Tampa Bay (formerly known as Busch Gardens Africa)* is a 335-acre 19th century African-themed animal park located in *Tampa*. It opened on March 31, 1959 as an admission-free hospitality facility for the *Tampa Anheuser-Busch* brewery on the grounds of the manufacturing plant.

• The *Tampa Anheuser-Busch* brewery closed some years later, and *Busch Gardens* focused progressively on its tropical landscape, exotic animals, and amusements. *Busch Gardens* began charging admission as the entertainment became more complex, with extra fees for the thrill rides, such as the roller coasters for which *Busch Gardens* is best known. The park is operated by *SeaWorld Parks & Entertainment*, owned by the private equity firm *The Blackstone Group*. In 2010, the park hosted 4.2 million people, placing in the Top 20 of the most-visited theme parks in the U.S. and in the Top 25 worldwide.

• In Season 6 of *The Bachelor* (2004), bachelor *Byron Velvick* chose bachelorette *Maribel Liliana "Mary" Delgado* of *Tampa*. Delgado, who came to the U.S. with her parents from Cuba when she was a year old, was also a contestant during the 4th season. Velvick asked Delgado to marry him in Spanish so her parents could understand his proposal. Delgado accepted.

• *Tampa* businesswoman *Tina Greene* and her husband *Ken* came in 2nd place for CBS's *Amazing Race* in 2008. The race spanned 23 days, five continents and nearly 40,000 miles. They missed the golden ring by mere seconds.

• *Angela Bassett* became well known for her biographical film roles portraying real life women in African American culture,

including *Tina Turner* in *What's Love Got to Do with It*, as well as *Betty Shabazz*, *Rosa Parks*, *Voletta Wallace* and *Katherine Jackson*. *Bassett* won a *Golden Globe* and earned an *Academy Award* nomination for her portrayal of Turner. She was the first African-American to win the Golden Globe Award for Best Actress. Bassett grew up in *St. Petersburg*, and attended *Boca Ciega High School.*

Angela Bassett

• In 2000, *Angela Bassett* turned down the lead role in *Monster's Ball;* the role earned *Halle Berry* the *Academy Award*.

• The *Third Seminole War* lasted from 1855 to 1858. At its end, U.S. forces estimated only 100 *Seminoles* were left in *Florida*. In 1859, 75 *Seminoles* surrendered and were sent to the West, but some *Seminoles* continued to live in the *Everglades*.

• *Marty Balin* (born Martyn Jerel Buchwald) is best known as the founder and lead singer of the psychedelic rock band *Jefferson Airplane*. Balin lives in *Temple Terrace, Florida*.

Anclote Key Lighthouse

• *Anclote Key lighthouse*, a picturesque 1887 light, sits on the southern tip of *Anclote Key*, off the coast of *Tarpon Springs*, at the mouth of the *Anclote River*. The area is well known for its sponges which are found on the bottom of the *Anclote River* and nearby places throughout the *Gulf of Mexico*.

• The word *Anclote* is a *Spanish* word meaning anchor. The island of *Anclote Key* is about 180 acres; around 4 miles long, less than a mile wide. The plural, *Anclote Keys* refers to the many smaller islands that lay on the island's northeastern side.

• Four islands with quiet sandy beaches make up the 403-acre *Anclote Key Preserve State Park; Anclote Key, North Anclote Bar, South Anclote Bar* and *Three Rooker Island*. Located three miles off the coast of *Tarpon Springs,* the park is accessible only by boat or ferry. The park is home to at least 43 species of birds, including the American oystercatcher and bald eagle.

• *Dunedin Fine Art Center* gained it roots in 1969 as a vision of the *Dunedin Junior Service League*, who recognized the importance of the arts to daily life, & resolved to work toward the creation of a cultural climate, and the eventual building of a fine arts and cultural center. Ground was broken on *The Dunedin Fine Art Center* in 1974.

• At the *Bishop Planetarium* (with a domed theater screen), in *Bradenton*, programs range from *black holes* to *Jimi Hendrix, Pink Floyd*, and other rockers.

• The *Bishop Planetarium* is a multipurpose, all-digital domed theater, boasting one of the most advanced projection systems in the world. Incorporating unidirectional stadium style seating and a digital 25,000 watt Dolby 5.1 surround sound system.

• The *Rock Hall of Fame* at *Bishop Planetarium* in *Bradenton* is forty-five minutes of classic rock and roll, including the *Doors, Led Zeppelin, Aerosmith and Pink Floyd* set to mind-boggling computer-generated animations on the planetarium's dome. *Rock Hall of Fame* is shown on the first Saturday night of each month at 8:15 pm, and seating capacity is 124 people.

• Founded in 1946 by community leaders, the *South Florida Museum* opened in 1947 on *Bradenton's Memorial Pier* with the *Montague Tallant* collection of *Florida's First Peoples*.

• In 1995, *The Florida Aquarium* opened its doors in *Tampa*, serving one million visitors and bringing a positive economic impact of $60-million to the community in its first year.

• Major League baseball player and manager *Tony La Russa* managed teams to six league championships and three *World Series* titles, and ranks third in all-time major league wins by a manager. *La Russa* was born in *Tampa*, graduated from the *University of South Florida* and earned a Juris Doctor (J.D.) degree from *Florida State University*. He was admitted to the Florida Bar in 1980; one of the very few major league managers ever who earned a law degree or passed a state bar exam. He retired from baseball three days after winning the *2011 World Series* title and after *33* seasons as major league manager.

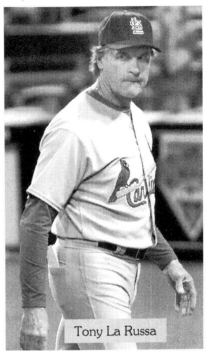
Tony La Russa

• Opened in January 2011, the *Dali Museum* in *St. Pete* quickly made *AOL Travel's list of "Buildings You Have to See Before You Die."* High-profile architect *Yann Weymouth* created the design to pay homage to Dali's free-flowing imagination. The structure represents the artist's blend of classical and fantastical styles. This downtown icon has 18" thick concrete walls that make up the 66,000-square-foot building while a seemingly fluid glass portion, known as "The Enigma", wraps around the building like one of Dali's melting clocks. The Helical Staircase is the main architectural focus of the interior and spirals from the ground to the third floor galleries. The building displays the work of Dali including a 2,000-piece permanent collection.

• *Roland Kent LaVoie*, better known as *Lobo*, was successful in the early 1970s, scoring several Top 10 hits, including *"Me and You and a Dog Named Boo"*, and *"I'd Love You to Want Me."* He grew up in *Winter Haven*, and got his musical start in 1964, while attending the *University of South Florida*. *LaVoie* joined a band called the *Sugar Beats*; released his first solo album in 1969, and became known as *Lobo* in 1971.

• *Anthony "Tony" Dungy* became the first African American head coach to win the *Super Bowl* when his *Colts* defeated the *Chicago Bears* in *Super Bowl XLI*. Dungy was head coach of the *Tampa Bay Buccaneers* from 1996 to 2001, was fired, and moved on to become head coach of the *Indianapolis Colts* (2002-08). He set the NFL record for consecutive playoff appearances by a head coach, and became the third man to win Super Bowls both as a player and a head coach, following *Mike Ditka* and *Tom Flores*. Dungy retired as the Colts coach after the 2008-09 season.

Gallagher

• *Leo Anthony Gallagher*, better known as the comedian who smashes watermelons, grew up in *South Tampa*. He attended *H. B. Plant High School*, and then graduated from the *University of South Florida* with a Chemical Engineering degree in 1970. After college, Gallagher became road manager for comic/musician *Jim Stafford*. But in 1969 *Gallagher* decided to take the stage himself.

• The *Territory of Florida* was a United States territory that existed from March 30, 1822, until March 3, 1845.

• *Seven Gables House* in *Heritage Park* *(southern Pinellas County)* is one of the most majestic examples of turn-of-the-century Victorian architecture. Built in 1907, this 13 room house was at one time used as a private club, a tea room, a boarding house and a parsonage. It was moved from a high bluff overlooking *Clearwater Bay* and floated down the intercoastal waterways to its present location in 1976.

Seven Gables

• *Heritage Village* is a 21-acre living history museum located in *Largo*. The natural pine and palmetto landscape is home to some of the Pinellas County's most historic buildings. Nearly 30 historic structures dating to the *McMullen Log House*, oldest structure in *Pinellas County;* including a school, railroad depot, sponge warehouse, church, store and several historic homes.

• *The Bounty*, a replica of the *HMS Bounty* made for the 1962 movie *Mutiny on the Bounty*, starring *Marlon Brando*, was permanently docked near the *St. Petersburg Pier* for many years until it was sold to *Ted Turner* in 1986. *The Bounty* still made winter visits to *St. Petersburg* until its dramatic sinking October 29, 2012 during Hurricane Sandy.

• A large settlement wave occurred 1923-26 in *Tampa*. Many subdivisions were built during this era; one of the most notable was *Davis Islands*, a man-made island created by *D.P. Davis* close to the main business district. The elegant homes Davis built are still some of *Tampa's* finest residences.

• *Davis Islands* is technically an archipelago, hence the plural form "Islands" in its name. Originally, *Davis Islands* consisted of three islands. With the construction of the airport, however, the end of one canal was filled in to make enough land area for a runway, connecting the two largest islands and reducing the archipelago's island count to two.

• *Tampa* native *D. P. Davis* dredged land for the development. He planned a resort community with three hotels, nine-hole golf course, airport, and swimming pool. Davis then sold 306 of the original lots for $1,683,582. The development stalled when the *Florida* land boom of the early 1920s wound down, and *Davis* was mysteriously lost at sea while making a transatlantic voyage in October 1926.

• In 2010, *USF* placed 9th among all universities worldwide in the number of U. S. patents granted. The university has an annual economic impact of $3.7 billion on the area.

• *Jennifer "Jenn" Sterger* of *Lutz*, was one of a group called the *FSU Cowgirls*, known for wearing skimpy clothing and cowboy hats to football games. She was shown on national TV during a 2005 Florida State–Miami football game, and announcer *Brent Musburger* commented that "*1,500 red-blooded Americans just decided to apply to Florida State.*" Her career took off; as a television personality, model as well as *Sports Illustrated* columnist. *Sterger* posed for both *Maxim* and *Playboy* magazines and was a spokesperson for *Sprint* and *Dr. Pepper*. She was named one of the *20 Hottest Women of the Web*, and was a featured Celeb on *E!: Entertainment Television*.

Jenn Sterger

• *Richard J. "Dick" Vitale*, also known as *"Dickie V"*, a basketball sportscaster, former head coach in both college and professional ranks, is a resident of *Lakewood Ranch, Florida*, near *Bradenton*. He is well known as a sportscaster for the enthusiastic and colorful remarks he makes during games. He has authored nine books and appeared in several movies, and in 2008 *Dick Vitale* was inducted into the *Basketball Hall of Fame*.

• The *Spanish-American War* was popular in *Ybor City*. Many of the Cuban cigar workers had long pressed for Cuba to be free of Spanish colonial rule. Leaders had come to *Tampa* many times to raise money and volunteers for the cause. With the U.S. entering the war to fight against Spain, it seemed that their dreams would actually be realized.

• Modeled after the *Doge's Palace* in *Venice* for *John and Mable Ringling's* winter home, *Ca'd'Zan* in *Sarasota* has been restored to its 1920s appearance. It was designed by architect Dwight James Baum and built of materials shipped from Europe.

• The 1998 film *Great Expectations*, directed by Alfonso Cuarón, had portions filmed at *Ca'd'Zan* mansion in *Sarasota*, which served as *Ms. Dinsmoor's house, Paradiso Perduto.*

• *Ca'd'Zan Gateway* is the entrance to the palatial home of *John and Mable Ringling* in *Sarasota*. This is Venetian dialect for *"House of John"* and is among the last of the grand eclectic "palaces" built by wealthy Americans in the late nineteenth and early twentieth centuries. Completed in 1926, its decorative elements derived from Italian Renaissance, Baroque, Venetian Gothic and modern architecture embellish this lovely mansion, which served as *John Ringling's* winter home.

• Through this arch *(Ca'd'Zan Gateway)* you enter the world of *John Ringling* (1866-1936) one of the greatest business tycoons and culture barons of his day. On his death he bequeathed his art collection and all property to the people of *Florida*, thus preserving the exuberant lifestyle of the roaring twenties.

• Completed in 1912, *Tampa Union Station* is listed on the *National Register of Historic Places*. Once vacant and boarded-up, *Union Station* is an active train station today. After a multi-year restoration in the 1990s, the building reopened to the public in May 1998, and serves more than 140,000 Amtrak passengers each year. It is owned by the *City of Tampa*.

Tampa Depot opened in 1912

• On May 12, 2012, on the occasion of the station's Centennial celebration and *National Train Day*, *Tampa Union Station* was officially added to the *National Register of Historic Railroad Landmarks* by the *National Railway Historical Society (NRHS)*. Officials of the NRHS presented a commemorative plaque to the station at their event to note this designation.

• *Temple Terrace* is a city in northeast *Hillsborough County*, adjacent to *Tampa*. It was named for the *Temple orange*, a new hybrid just created when *Temple Terrace* was being formed. The "terrace" part of the name refers to the terraced terrain of the area by the river where the city was founded.

• The *Temple orange* is a cross between the mandarin orange (tangerine) and the common sweet orange. It was named after Florida-born *William Chase Temple*, one-time owner of the *Pittsburgh Pirates*. He was first president of the *Florida Citrus Exchange*. *Temple Terrace* was the first place in the U.S. where the new *Temple orange* was grown in large quantities.

• *Tampa's* economy is founded on a diverse base that includes tourism, agriculture, construction, government, technology, finance, health care, and the *Port of Tampa*.

• *Snooty*, a male manatee 9 feet 7 inches long, weighing over 1,200 pounds, is the oldest manatee in captivity. He is the headliner at the *South Florida Museum and Parker Manatee Aquarium* at *Bradenton*.

• Born July 21, 1948, at the old *Miami Aquarium and Tackle Company, Snooty* was the first manatee born in captivity. He was brought to *Bradenton* for the *1949 Desoto Celebration*. Each year visitors help *Snooty* celebrate his birthday at a free *Birthday Bash and Wildlife Awareness Festival;* since he was the first manatee to have an actual recorded birth date!

• The *Parker Manatee Aquarium* opened in 1993, with above and below water viewing capabilities, a medical pool, an exhibition area and a 60,000-gallon tank for *Snooty* and his additional manatee friends.

• In August 2001, an electrical fire destroyed the *Bishop Planetarium* in *Bradenton*, and severely damaged a state-of-the-art education wing and all of the museum's administrative areas. In September 2002, the museum re-opened the first floor with new exhibits and gallery. A new education wing was re-opened in March 2004 and the new state-of-the-science planetarium and theater opened to the public in June 2005.

• Two university hospitals, *H. Lee Moffitt Cancer Center* and *USF Psychiatry Center*, as well as the college of public health, were built during the 1980s by the *University of South Florida*.

• The *Marshall Center* at the *University of South Florida* is the largest university student center in the state of *Florida*.

• On August 18, 2010, *St. Petersburg City Council* accepted *Mayor Bill Foster's* recommendation to demolish the current *Pier* building. On January 20, 2012, the *St. Petersburg Pier Competition Jury* unanimously selected Michael Maltzan Architecture's *The Lens* as the design for the new pier, and the 1973 Pier was scheduled to close May 31, 2013.

• The *St. Petersburg Pier* dates back to 1889, when the *Orange Belt Railway* constructed the *Railroad Pier on Tampa Bay* as a railway-accessible sightseeing and recreational resort for locals and tourists. The *Pier* actually pre-dates the 1892 incorporation of *St. Petersburg* as a city by three years.

• After the sudden death of *Thomas Rowe*, *The Don CeSar* in *St. Petersburg* fell into disrepair until the *United States* entered into *World War II* and the hotel was bought by the Army and converted into a military hospital (1942). In 1945 it was converted into a *Veterans Administration Regional Office.*

• In March 1972 the *Don CeSar* was sold to *C. L. Pyatt* and *William Bowman Jr.*, who renovated the facility back into a hotel. Multiple renovations have updated and added on to the hotel, including a 4,000-square-foot spa, a signature restaurant, and a second outdoor swimming pool. After the addition of the full-service beach club and spa, the official name of the hotel was changed to *The Don CeSar Beach Resort and Spa*.

• *Tampa,* county seat of *Hillsborough County*, is the 54th largest city in the nation; third most populous city in *Florida*. It is located on the west coast of *Florida*, approximately 200 miles northwest of *Miami,* 275 south of *Tallahassee,* 180 southwest of *Jacksonville,* and 20 miles northeast of *St. Petersburg.*

• The *Tarpon Springs* community has the highest percentage of *Greek Americans* of any city in the entire United States.

• *Billy Graham* attended *Florida Bible Institute*, which owned the property in *Temple Terrace* now occupied by *Florida College* in the late 1930s. He says he received his "calling" on the 18th green of the *Temple Terrace Golf and Country Club.* A *Billy Graham Memorial Park* now includes that site.

• The 1953 movie *Beneath the 12-Mile Reef,* depicts sponge diving. It takes place and was filmed in *Tarpon Springs*.

• *Philippe Park* in *Safety Harbor* includes an Indian mound listed in the *National Register of Historic Landmarks*. Majestic trees welcome visitors at the oldest park in *Pinellas County* along a one-mile length of shoreline on *Old Tampa Bay*.

• Formerly known as the *"Old Gandy Bridge,"* the 2.6-mile *Friendship Trail Bridge* over beautiful *Tampa Bay* connects *Pinellas County* to *Tampa*. It offers a unique experience for bicyclists, skaters, joggers and fishermen. It is open daily from dawn to dusk. There is no charge; or, shade from the sun.

• *Ruth Eckerd Hall* is one of the outstanding theaters that characterize the *Clearwater* area. Constructed in 1983 by the *Frank Lloyd Wright Foundation*, at the *Richard Baumgardner Center for the Performing Arts*, it is well known and respected for its acoustics and state-of-the-art equipment and offers a wide range of performances for every age and musical taste.

• *Winter* is a Dolphin that was found injured inside a crab trap. At only 80 pounds and just 4 months old she was taken to the *Clearwater Marine Aquarium* for rehabilitation. It was soon discovered that *Winter* would lose her tail; however, a doctor was able to miraculously fit her with a prosthetic tail. *Hollywood* learned of this incredible story, and decided to film her journey. Released in the Fall of 2011 *Dolphin Tale* is the true story of *Winter's* survival and her heart-warming adventure.

• *Clearwater Marine Aquarium's* most notorious resident, *Winter* the dolphin, stars alongside *Morgan Freeman, Ashley Judd,* and *Harry Connick Jr.,* in *Dolphin Tale*, the 3D motion picture about her extraordinary life. Following the success of the film *Clearwater Marine Aquarium* expanded into the *Historic Downtown Clearwater's Harborview Center.* A shell of a former department store was transformed into *"Winter's Dolphin Tale Adventure,"* and visitors can see the "tailless" *Winter* in action.

• The city of *St. Petersburg* featured a world-famous *Madame Tussaud Wax Museum* from 1963 until 1989.

Esther Williams

• The *Esther Williams at Cypress Gardens* television spectacular on August 8, 1960 is still regarded as one of the most successful TV programs in history. More than half of all the television sets in the U. S. were tuned in to watch the *Cypress Gardens* special. In 1966, *Williams* was inducted into the *International Swimming Hall of Fame*. *Cypress Gardens*, the state's oldest theme park opened in 1936 and played host to 50 million people before closing in 2009.

• *Cypress Gardens* near *Winter Haven* was known as the *"Water Ski Capital of the World"* because many of the sport's landmark firsts and over 50 world records broken there.

• *Boca Ciega Millennium Park* in *Seminole* features a 35-foot wooden observation tower that offers a panoramic view of *Boca Ciega Bay*. A wide variety of birds flock to this park. Besides a special bird viewing area, visitors can fish off piers, launch a canoe or kayak, or picnic under a shelter.

• In 2005, *Fort De Soto* was rated the number one beach in America by the annual *Dr. Beach* rankings. *Trip Advisor* had the beach ranked number one in the nation for 2008. It is consistently rated as one of the nation's top beaches.

• *Sawgrass Lake Park* in *St. Petersburg* includes one of the largest maple swamps on the *Gulf Coast*. A boardwalk winds a mile through the lush environment to reveal birds, butterflies and alligators. The park is mentioned by the *National Audubon Society* as one of the premier birding sites in *Florida*.

• Long-time Tampa resident *Terry Gene Bollea*, better known by his ring name *Hulk Hogan*, was inducted into the *WWE Hall of Fame* in 2005. He is 12-time world champ; being a six-time WWF/WWE Champion and six-time WCW World Heavyweight Champion.

Hulk Hogan

• Professional wrestler, actor, and television personality, *Hulk Hogan* was also a skilled musician. He played bass guitar in several Florida-based rock bands, and dropped out of the *University of South Florida* before receiving a degree in order to pursue his music career. His band called *Ruckus* in the late 1970s, was quite the local sensation in the *Tampa Bay* region.

• *Hulk Hogan*, considered by many as the greatest pro wrestler of all time, starred in a reality TV series, *Hogan Knows Best*, which featured *Tampa Bay*. The show was produced by *Pink Sneakers Productions* and centered on the family life of wrestler *Hulk Hogan* (Terry Bollea). The series premiered July 10, 2005 with the largest audience for a VH1 premiere ever. During its four season run, the show was seen on 3 other networks in the United States, and in 14 countries around the world.

Willis Fish Cabin

• *West Coast Fishing Company Residential Cabin, Willis Fish Cabin and Ice Station* was built in *Charlotte Harbor*, near *Port Charlotte* on the west coast of *Florida*, around 1920 by Claude Willis, an oysterman from Charlotte Harbor. This simple frame structure with metal roof, sits high above the water on stilts.

• Buildings to house fishermen, with a place to process fish, were a very important part of *Charlotte Harbor*. Many such buildings were portable structures that moved to various locations throughout the harbor.

• In the early 1900s over 300 people worked in the commercial fishing industry in Charlotte Harbor.

•The Charlotte Harbor commercial fishing industry was one of the largest operations in Florida during the first half of the twentieth century. "Run Boats" regularly brought ice and supplies from the Punta Gorda Ice Plant to keep the fish catch on ice. The iced fish was brought back to Punta Gorda on the run boats for processing and shipping.

• Ice houses were also situated throughout the area on stilts, where the fish catches were stored. The fish were iced and stored in rooms with double-thick Cypress walls.

• *Florida Bible Institute* was founded in 1932, in *Temple Terrace*, by *Dr. William T. Watson*, a fundamentalist preacher from North Carolina and pastor of a large Christian and Missionary Alliance church in *St. Petersburg*. The name was changed again in 1947 to *Trinity College of Florida*, and re-located to *New Port Richey*. It is a private college, and has always been distinctly interdenominational. The property in *Temple Terrace* was sold to the newly formed *Florida College*.

• The *Tampa Bay Hotel* has six minarets, four cupolas, and three domes. In the early 1990s, all were restored to their original stainless steel state.

• *St. Petersburg* is the fourth most populous city in the state of *Florida* and the largest city in the state that is not a county seat. *St. Petersburg* is the second largest city in the *Tampa Bay Area*, which is composed of roughly 2.8 million residents.

• *St. Petersburg* became the birthplace of scheduled aviation on December 17, 1913, when *Tom Benoist* signed the world's first commercial airline contract with the *City of St. Petersburg* - 10 years to the day after the Wright brothers had first flown successfully at Kitty Hawk. The agreement called for two scheduled flights daily between *St. Petersburg* and *Tampa*, six days a week in his Airboat.

• The original *Sunshine Skyway Bridge* is featured in the original opening credits to the 1988 *Superboy* television series which showed the hero flying over the damaged original span and then turning to view the new bridge under construction.

• Tampa's *Lowry Park Zoological Society*, in agreement with the *City of Tampa*, operates *Lowry Park Zoo* as a nonprofit charitable organization.

• One of the nation's most popular shock jocks hails from the *Tampa Bay* area. He is known as *Bubba the Love Sponge* . His outrageous on-air antics and controversial language got *Bubba Clem* of *Tierra Verde* booted from terrestrial radio, only to see him launch a raunchier *Sirius* show on *Howard Stern's 101* channel; he returned to local airwaves in 2008.

• Part of the movie *Edward Scissorhands* was filmed on Tinsmith Circle in *Lutz*. This 1990 romantic fantasy film starring *Johnny Depp* was directed by *Tim Burton*. The majority of filming took place in the *Tampa Bay* Area, and generated over $6 million for the local economy. In the credits the town is named in the *"Thank you"* section.

• *Lutz, Florida* and the *Southgate Shopping Center* of *Lakeland* were chosen for a three month shooting schedule for the filming of *Edward Scissorhands*. The facade of the Gothic mansion was built outside of Dade City. Production then moved to a *Fox Studios* sound stage in Century City, California, for filming interior shots.

• According to the *World Atlas USA*, *Hernando County* is the geographic center of *Florida*. The highest point in the county is *Chinsegut Hill* at an elevation of 269 feet. The low point of the county is 0 feet at the coastline of the *Gulf of Mexico*.

• *St. Petersburg* is often referred to by locals as *St. Pete*. However, neighboring *St. Pete Beach* officially shortened its name in 1994 after a vote by its residents.

• The city of *St. Petersburg* was co-founded by *John Williams*, formerly of *Detroit*, who purchased the land in 1876, and by *Peter Demens*, who was instrumental in bringing the terminus of a railroad there in 1888. The city was incorporated on February 29, 1892, with a population of some 300 people.

• Co-founders of the new city at the very end of the *Pinellas Peninsula, John C. Williams* and *Peter Demens*, flipped a coin to see who would have the honor of naming the city. Demens won the toss and named the city after his birthplace and early home, *Saint Petersburg, Russia*. Williams named the first hotel after his birthplace, *Detroit* (a hotel built by Demens). The *Detroit Hotel* has been turned into a condominium.

• *Boyd Hill Nature Park*, located on *Lake Maggiore* in *St. Pete*, is a 245-acre preserve where one can see many endangered plants and rare wildlife of *Tampa Bay*. There is a bird exhibit which houses bald eagles, owls, hawks, and other species.

• *St. Petersburg* is located on a peninsula between *Tampa Bay* and the *Gulf of Mexico*. It is connected to mainland *Florida* to the north; with the city of *Tampa* to the east by causeways and bridges across *Tampa Bay*; and to *Bradenton* in the south by the *Sunshine Skyway Bridge* (Interstate 275).

• In 1763, *Spain* traded *Florida* to the *Kingdom of Great Britain* for control of *Havana, Cuba*, which had been captured by the *British*. During the *American Revolutionary War*, the *Spanish*, allied with the *French* (who were actively at war with Britain). As part of the *Treaty of Paris* in 1784, ending the *Revolutionary War,* all of *Florida* was returned to *Spanish* control.

• *Henry B. Plant's* 1884 railroad extension to the *Hillsborough River* provided access to new areas, and he built lavish hotels along his rail line to attract visitors into *Tampa Bay*.

• *Trans Canada Airlines* inaugurated international flights in 1950 at *Tampa's Drew Field,* and the airport was renamed *Tampa International Airport*. The second terminal was quickly planned and opened in 1952 near the intersection of Columbus Drive and West Shore Blvd.

• In continuous operation since being dedicated in 1916, the *St. Petersburg Open Air Post Office* is the nation's first open-air post office. This Italian-inspired architecture building has highly ornamental archways, intricate metal work, terra cotta piers and a Spanish tile roof that all contribute to making this landmark an important Mediterranean Revival building. The American eagle and gargoyles blend into the design. The building was listed on the *National Register of Historic Places* in 1975.

• Philadelphia publisher *F. A. Davis* turned on *St. Petersburg's* first electrical service in 1897 and its first trolley service in 1904.

• By 1860, *Tampa* had become a market town for the entire inland region - its protected river location on the West Coast's largest harbor made in a good location for trade. However, the *Civil War* ended that situation, and *Union* gunboats entering *Tampa Bay*, turned *Tampa* into a semi-deserted town.

• Before the *Sunshine Skyway Bridge* linked *Pinellas County* to *Manatee County*, big name ballplayers such as *Ted Williams, Joe DiMaggio* and *Yogi Berra* travelled on the *Bee Line Ferry* across *Tampa Bay* for spring training camps on the Gulf coast. There were even special trips on the *Bee Line Ferry* for the *Ringling Circus* animals heading north for the summer circuit.

• *Brian Johnson* of Sarasota, a singer and lyricist who has been the lead singer for the rock band *AC/DC* since 1980, was inducted into the *Rock and Roll Hall of Fame* in 2003, along with the other members of the band.

• *Julian Barnes Lane* was inducted into the *University of Florida Athletic Hall of Fame* in 1990. Lane was the 45th mayor of *Tampa*, and served as a member of the *Florida Legislature*. He was born in *Tampa*, and graduated from *Hillsborough High School*. Lane played football for the *Florida Gators* 1934 to 1936.

Brian Johnson

• Comedian, musician *Jim Stafford* was raised in *Winter Haven*. In high school, he played in a band along with friends *Bobby Braddock, Kent LaVoie (also known as Lobo)* **and** *Gram Parsons (of the Byrds)*. Prominent in the 1970s, *Stafford* is self-taught on guitar, fiddle, piano, banjo, organ and harmonica. In 1967 and 1968, Stafford performed regularly and served as head writer/producer for the *Smothers Brothers Comedy Hour*. His highest ranking single was *Spiders and Snakes*, in 1974. *The Jim Stafford Show* was a six-week summer variety series on ABC in 1975.

• *Lowell 'Bud' Paxson* and *Roy Speer* launched the *Home Shopping Club* in 1982, a local cable channel seen on *Vision Cable* and *Group W Cable* in *Pinellas County*. It expanded into the first national shopping network three years later in 1985, changing its name to *HSN*, and pioneering the concept of a televised sales pitch for consumer goods and services.

- *Billy Mays*, well-known television Pitchman, was found unresponsive by his wife in his *Tampa* home in 2009. Prior to his death, Mays had signed a contract with *Taco Bell* to film infomercial-style TV commercials. Shooting was to begin in August 2009. Mays was scheduled for hip replacement surgery the day after he was found dead. Mays was only 50 years of age. Pallbearers for his funeral wore blue shirts and khaki pants, much like Mays wore when he advertised his products. Mays often mentioned proudly that he lived in *Odessa, Florida*.

Billy Mays

- *Home Shopping Network* or *HSN* is a 24-hour/7 day a week home shopping television network based in *St. Petersburg.* The corporate headquarters, studio and broadcasting facilities are all housed there. *HSN* has sister channels in several countries, and is televised via cable, satellite, and terrestrial channels, as well as an online outlet at HSN.com, and catalog company.

- On January 28, 2010 *President Barack Obama* became the first sitting president to visit the *University of Tampa* campus.

• Several ZIP Codes serve *Lutz* and the surrounding areas; 33548, 33549, 33558 and 33559. These zip codes extend north past the *Hillsborough County* line to State Road 54 into southern *Pasco County*. That area is also called *Lutz*, and often referred to as *Pasco Lutz* by residents and newspapers.

• In April 2008, 15 patas monkeys escaped from *Safari Wild*, an animal attraction in rural *Polk County*. The park was owned and operated by long-time *Lowry Park Zoo* director *Lex Salisbury*. Investigations revealed questionable transactions between *Safari Wild* and *Lowry Park Zoo*. In 2008, Salisbury resigned from his position at the zoo under pressure from the zoo's board of directors and the city of *Tampa*. In 2009 they agreed upon a settlement; but *Salisbury* did not admit to any wrongdoing.

• The *Seaboard Air Line Railway* passenger depot in 1922 was located along today's East Street, just north of Court Street in *Clearwater*. The *Tampa and Gulf Coast Railway* added this line to *Pinellas* in 1914, but *Seaboard* put its name on the line soon after. When the 1924 depot was built a bit further south, this became the freight depot. This route is still used by *CSX*.

• Originally known as *The Sunshine City* with an annual 361 days of sunshine each year, *St. Petersburg* holds a *Guinness World Record* for the most consecutive days of sunshine - a stretch lasting 768 days that began in 1967.

• Situated in *Hernando County*, on the second highest elevation in peninsular *Florida*, the manor house for *Chinsegut Hill* was expanded to its majesty by *Col. Raymond Robins,* who bought the property in 1904. Parts of the house were built in 1849.

Chinsegut Hill

• *Chinsegut* is an Indian word interpreted liberally by *Raymond Robins* as "A place where things of true value that have been lost may be found again."

• The *University of Florida* conferred the honorary *Doctor of Law* degree upon *Col. Raymond Robins* under the regal *Altar Oak* on his *Chinsegut Hill Estate* in *Hernando County*, and it is here that he and his wife rest. Ironically, *Chinsegut Hill* is now run as a *Conference Center* by the *University of South Florida*.

• *Polk County* remains even today as an almost mystical place of lakes and orange groves, of small towns and commercial centers. Squeezed between *Tampa* and *Orlando*, the area is experiencing more growth than it ever has in the past. More and More people are discovering the charm of *Polk County*.

• The *Gandy Bridge*, conceived by *George Gandy,* opened in 1924. It was the first causeway to be built across *Tampa Bay*, connecting *St. Petersburg* and *Tampa* without a circuitous 43-mile trip around the bay through *Oldsmar*.

• *Jim Courier*, former world number 1 professional tennis player from *Dade City (Pasco County)*, founded *Courier's Kids*, a non-profit organization to supports tennis programs in the inner city of *St. Petersburg*. It is a program for kids 10 years old and under who have not had any previous tennis instruction.

• *Jennifer Capriati* of *Wesley Chapel (Pasco County)* was inducted into the *International Tennis Hall of Fame* in 2012. *Capriati* is a former world number one ranked professional tennis player. She made her professional debut in 1990 at the age of 13. *Capriati* became the youngest player to crack the top 10 at age 14. Between 1990-1993, she won six singles titles, including a Gold Medal at the *1992 Barcelona Olympics*; she won 14 professional tourneys during her career.

Jennifer Capriati

• Rural *Dade City*, known mostly for its strawberries, is home to an unusual 50-acre *Giraffe Ranch*, that resembles an African preserve, including zebras, an impala, ostriches, a pair of pygmy hippos, and many other animal species roaming free on the grounds.

• *Giraffe Ranch* is not a zoo or theme park, it is a working ranch that specializes in exotic species as well as domestic animals like their small herd of *Austrian Haflinger* horses and the tiny *Irish Dexter* cattle. However, it is open to the public as an educational adventure. Expert guides provide tours in specially designed 4-wheel drive vehicles or by camel-backed safari to explain conservation efforts to help preserve species that are endangered or extinct in the wild.

• Located in beautiful east *Pasco County* 45 minutes north of *Tampa,* the *Giraffe Ranch* is adjoining *Florida's* second largest wilderness area, the *Green Swamp*. With huge live oaks, native orchids, lush pastures and ephemeral wetlands, the ranch is also a native wildlife preserve. Every night up to 200 sandhill cranes roost on the grounds.

• Family-owned and operated for over 13 years, *Giraffe Ranch* in *Dade City* is a *Florida* agritourism enterprise; open by reservation only. They offer two tours each day at 11 a.m. and 2 p.m. Tours (educational adventures) are strictly limited in size.

• At 7 feet tall, weighing 411 pounds, *Paul Wight "The Big Show"* from Odessa, is billed as "The World's Largest Athlete." Wight is a professional wrestler and actor. He is a six-time world champion; the first person ever to hold all four championships, and the youngest to ever win the *WCW World Heavyweight Champion* title.

Paul Wight

• In 1942, the privately owned *Bee Line Ferry*, operating from *St. Pete* to *Piney Point* near present-day *Port Manatee*, ceased operations after the federal government requisitioned its boats for the war effort. Automobiles and trucks had to detour 50 miles inland via *Gandy Bridge*.

• One of the ferries which operated from *St. Pete* to *Piney Point*, the *"Pinellas"*, was built in Wilmington, DE in 1882 to operate on the *Cape Fear River* in 1890 between Wilmington, NC and the beaches. Brought to *Florida* in 1926, she was converted into a diesel ferry. Her name was changed to the *Seabrook* during *WWII* when she became part of the US Navy. After the War, she returned to her ferry runs, and when the ferry operation closed, the heroic ferry was turned into a fishing excursion boat.

• The *Tampa Bay Area* is the nation's 14th largest television market; served by fourteen local broadcast television stations, as well as a variety of cable-only local stations. More than 70 FM and AM stations make it the nation's 19th largest radio market.

• *Pinellas County* was formed in 1912. It was separated from *Hillsborough County* and took the name of the peninsula it covers. The name *Pinellas* was derived from the Spanish *"Punta Pinal"* meaning *Point of Pines*. The *Old Pinellas County Courthouse* was designed by pioneer, *Tampa* Architect, *Francis Kennard*. The first phase of construction was completed in 1917. The second phase in 1926. It is actually the second one built in *Clearwater*. The first *Pinellas County Courthouse* was located on the present site of the Peace Memorial Church, and built in a few hours to establish Clearwater as the county seat.

• Still a distinguished landmark in *Clearwater,* the *Old Pinellas County Courthouse* is listed on the *National Register of Historic Places* for both its historic value, and architectural significance.

• *Joanie Laurer* finished her last year of high school in *Spain*, and then attended the *University of Tampa*, graduating with a major in Spanish Literature. Known professionally as *Chyna,* she was a professional wrestler, actress, pornographic actress and bodybuilder. She is best known for her career with the *World Wrestling Federation (WWF)* from 1997 to 2001, where she was billed as *Chyna: The Ninth Wonder of the World.*

• In an unusual agreement in 1975, the *New College* Board of Trustees in *Sarasota* agreed to hand over the campus and other assets to the state, at the time valued at $8.5 million, if the state agreed to operate the school as a separate unit within the *University of South Florida*, (USF). The New College 144-acre bay front campus is approximately fifty miles south of *Tampa*.

• The *Overseas Railroad*, also known as the *Key West Extension* of the *Florida East Coast Railway*, was heavily damaged in the *Labor Day Hurricane* of 1935. The *Florida East Coast Railway* was financially unable to rebuild the destroyed sections, so the roadbed and remaining bridges were sold to the *State of Florida*, which built the Overseas Highway to Key West, using much of the remaining railway infrastructure. Key West is located 128 miles beyond the end of the Florida peninsula.

Overseas Railroad
Key West Extension

• The *Orange Belt Railway* was a narrow gauge railway running from *St. Pete* through *Odessa,* and *Ehren* to *Trilby, Florida.* It was used primarily to haul logs and lumber, and occasionally passengers. It was also known as the *Sanford & St. Petersburg,* and was absorbed by the *Plant Railway* in 1895.

• Author *Dennis Lehane* has written several award-winning novels, including bestsellers *Mystic River, Gone, Baby, Gone,* and *Shutter Island* that were adapted into major movies. *Lehane* is a graduate of *Eckerd College (St. Petersburg),* where he says he found his passion for writing. Lehane was presented an honorary *Doctor of Humane Letters* degree from *Eckerd College* in 2005, and appointed to their Board of Trustees. He maintains a residence in *St. Petersburg,* and teaches as *writer-in-residence* at *Eckerd.* He also co-directs their noted *Writers in Paradise* conference each January.

Dennis Lehane

• *Myrtle* was an early settlement in *Pasco County* founded in 1893, about 3 miles northeast of *Stemper.* The name came from the large number of Myrtle trees there. The post office was established July 24, 1893 and operated until October 15, 1914. After the *Myrtle* post office closed, residents received mail at *Lutz.*

• *University of South Florida* emerged as a major research institution during the 1980s under the presidency of *John Lott Brown,* who also recruited basketball coach *Lee Rose,* one of the most popular coaches in *Bulls* history.

• The *South Florida Bulls* compete in *NCAA Division I;* a member of the *Big East Conference*, since 2005. Its marching band, the *Herd of Thunder* formed in 1999.

• The historic *Belleview Biltmore Resort and Spa* is situated on *Old Clearwater Bay*, with views of the bay and the barrier islands which border the *Gulf of Mexico*. The hotel was built in 1897 by railroad tycoon *Henry B. Plant* and was added to the *National Register of Historic Places* on December 26, 1979.

Belleview Biltmore

• The *Belleview Biltmore Resort* is thought to be the site of ghost sightings and other paranormal events. It was featured in a segment on the *Weird Travels* series on the *Travel Channel* television network; filmed in March 2004.

• *University of South Florida* played its 1st football game in 1997.

• In 2012, the *Tampa Bay Times Forum* was ranked second in the United States (15th in the world) by *Pollstar* magazine and ninth in the U.S. (14th in the world) by *Venues Today Magazine*. Rankings are based on concert ticket sales, events and family shows in venues seating more than 15,000 people.

• *Hernando County* is home to the largest *Wal-Mart Distribution Center* (truck-to-truck) in the U.S. approximately 1,600,000 square feet in size and located in *Ridge Manor*.

• *Florida Aquarium's Brews By The Bay* features *Oktoberfest* brews & craft beers from *Pepin Distributing*. It is the annual beer & food festival, featuring over 85 different types of beer, excellent food from bay area restaurants and live entertainment!

• *Dunedin Depot* sits prominently alongside the *Pinellas Trail* in downtown *Dunedin*. It houses a museum of memorabilia from early Dunedin and vicinity. This section of the *Pinellas Trail* has become a favorite for trail travelers. The original track laid through *Dunedin* in 1888 was narrow gauge, a part of the *Orange Belt Railroad* built by *Peter Demens*. The *Dunedin Depot* was built in the early 1920s on the site of the original station, constructed in 1888. After the railroad service stopped, the old train station was abandoned. The restoration was undertaken as a project by the *Dunedin Historical Society*. In 1981 the renewed facility was dedicated as their museum. A final passenger train run was made in 1987 from *St. Petersburg* to *Tarpon Springs*. The tracks were then removed, and the *Pinellas Trail* occupies the historic track bed.

Dunedin Depot

• When a red tide algae bloom wiped out sponge fields in the *Gulf of Mexico* in 1947, spongers in *Tarpon Springs* dropped hundreds of sponge disks in the *Gulf of Mexico* in an attempt to cultivate sponges. A sponge disk is 10 inches in diameter, made of concrete and has four holes in the middle. Live sponges were tied onto the disks, wrapped in heavy burlap and dropped in rows off the small island of *Anclote Key.* This method worked, but was too expensive, and took too long to produce a salable sponge; it was eventually abandoned.

• *Freeman H. Horton*, the civil engineer who first proposed a bridge across *Tampa Bay* to *Palmetto,* was born in *Fogartyville*, a *Bradenton* community. *Horton* was the first *Manatee County High School* student to graduate in civil engineering from the *Massachusetts Institute of Technology* and *Harvard University*.

• *USF Polytechnic* was established in 1988 as *USF Lakeland*. It serves more than 2,000 students offering over 20 complete undergraduate and graduate degrees in the areas of arts and sciences, business, education, engineering, and information technology. In 2012, *USF Polytechnic* became *Florida Polytechnic University*, the 12th member institution of the State University System.

• The *Jennings Estate* was the home of *Brooksville's* only resident elected *Governor of Florida*. It was also home of the founders of the world famous *Christmas House. William S. Jennings* built this house shortly after arriving in *Florida* from Illinois in 1886. It is modeled after the Governor's mansion in *Tallahassee*. A former *Hernando County Judge* and speaker of the *State House*, *Jennings* was nominated as a candidate for governor in 1900, after 44 ballots. *William Jennings Bryan*, his cousin and Democrat candidate for president, visited here during his presidential campaign. It served as the *Christmas House* in 1970, until it moved to its present location.

• The first post office at *Lutz* was a 7-square-foot building on a lot south of the depot. *George Sibthorpe*, the first postmaster of *Lutz*, moved the post office to his realty office. In 1914, the post office was again moved to inside the train depot.

• History was made in *Tampa* August 27, 2012 when the 40th *Republican National Convention* opened on schedule and immediately went into recess for a day because of *Tropical Storm Isaac*. The more than 70,000 people who descended upon the *Bay* area included 2,286 delegates and 2,125 alternate delegates from all 50 states, the *District of Columbia* and five U.S. territories.

John Cena

• *John Cena* is an actor and pro wrestler who lives in Tampa. *Cena* has won 19 championships, including 12 world titles (including the *WWE Championship* a record 10 times), yet he is best known world-wide (to all except the die-hard wrestling fans) as an *Action Star* in the movies.

• In its final operating year, the *Bee Line Ferry* carried 99,000 vehicles between *Pinellas County* and *Manatee County*. A bridge was deemed necessary because the estimate data projected the volume of traffic as high as 4,000 cars daily. The actual traffic count across the *Sunshine Skyway Bridge* averages more than ten times that number with over 50,000 vehicles per day.

• *University of South Florida* (USF) was founded in 1956, but the university was not officially named until the following year, and courses did not begin until 1960. Most popular of the names proposed for the new school were *Sunshine State University, Citrus State University, The University of the Western Hemisphere,* and *The University of Florida at Temple Terrace.*

• *Northwest Airlines* and *National Airlines* brought the *Jumbo Jet* to *Tampa International* in 1971 with the introduction of the *Boeing 747* and *McDonnell Douglas DC-10. Eastern Air Lines* brought the *Lockheed Tristar* to *TIA* a year later.

• *Tampa Int'l Airport* handled 16,732,051 passengers in 2011.

• *Tampa Bay* is home to more than 500 bottlenose dolphins and is one of the best places in *Florida* to view endangered manatees and numerous species of birds, many of which are threatened or endangered. All of this wildlife thrives in one of the busiest deepwater ports in the Southern United States.

• *Florida Aquarium* offers a 90-minute eco-tour around *Tampa Bay* on *Bay Spirit II,* a 72-foot catamaran. The *Wild Dolphin Cruise* at *The Florida Aquarium* earned the *Dolphin SMART* recognition in 2011.

• *Land O' Lakes* was created in 1949 when the towns of *Denham* and *Drexel* voted to change their names and become one community. The *Pasco County Historical Preservation Committee* decided to use 1950 as the town marker because that was the year the *Ehren* post office closed and the *Land O' Lakes* post office was opened.

• The one hundred-ten room *Fenway Hotel* overlooking the scenic *Gulf of Mexico* in *Dunedin* was completed in 1927. It was home to the first radio station in *Pinellas County*.

• *Fenway Hotel* is a historic Jazz Age hotel building overlooking *St. Joseph's Sound* on the *Gulf of Mexico* in *Dunedin*. It was built in 1924 and remained open until 1961 when it became *Trinity College*. Trinity College moved to *Pasco County* in 1988. It was purchased by *Schiller International University* in 1991. *SIU* moved their main campus to *Largo,* and the *Fenway* with 6.4 acres was purchased (in 2006) by *St. Petersburg* attorney *George Rahdert*, with plans to convert the structure into a 150-room historic condominium and hotel complex.

The Fenway Hotel

• The *Sports Hall of Fame* at *University of Tampa* includes former *NFL* player *John Matuszak* of the *Oakland Raiders,* who was also an actor and participated in the *World's Strongest Man* competition. As an actor, he is probably most remembered as *Sloth* in *The Goonies* (1985).

• *Lutz* began with the construction of a small train depot on the *Tampa Northern Railroad* which carried materials from *Tampa* to *Brooksville*. It was named *Lutz Station* by *William Paul Lutz,* an engineer on the *Tampa Northern Railroad*. The area surrounding the depot officially became known as *Lutz* when the U. S. Postal Service authorized a post office.

• The *Lutz Junction* was demolished in the late 1960s. A replica of the depot was rebuilt in the approximate location in 2000. The post office's structure is still in the same place today, although it is now an art gallery. A public library is located behind the train depot replica.

• The 227-foot tall Air Traffic Control Tower at *Tampa International Airport* became operational on July 15, 1972 and at the time was the tallest in the United States.

• *Manatees* can be viewed in the underwater observatory at *Homosassa Springs State Wildlife Park*. Most of the park's residents are injured animals undergoing rehabilitation. The notable exception is *Lucifer,* an African hippopotamus. When a permanent home could not be found for the retired actor, *Gov. Lawton Chiles* made *Lucifer* an honorary citizen of the state.

• The *Tampa Bay* area includes 24 square miles of inland waterways in *Hillsborough County* alone.

• Tallahassee was created as the capital of Florida during the second legislative session. It was chosen because it was roughly equidistant from St. Augustine and Pensacola, which had been the capitals of the Spanish colonies of East Florida and West Florida, respectively. The first session of Florida's Legislative Council - as a territory of the United States - met on July 22, 1822 at Pensacola and members from St. Augustine traveled fifty-nine days by water to attend.

'Cannonball' Adderley

• "Mercy Mercy Mercy" was a surprise hit for jazz musician *Julian "Cannonball" Adderley* on the Billboard charts in 1966, and it became a crossover pop hit. *Adderley* was born in *Tampa* in 1928, and became quite popular as a jazz saxophonist. *Adderley* died of a stroke in 1975, and was inducted that same year into the *Jazz Hall of Fame*.

• *Nat (Nathaniel) Adderley*, a jazz trumpet player, was born in 1931 in *Tampa*. He was the brother of saxophonist Julian "Cannonball" Adderley. *Nat* and *Cannonball* played with *Ray Charles* in the early 1940s, and his son *Nat Adderley, Jr.* a keyboardist, was long time musical director for *Luther Vandross*.

• *Citrus County* was first occupied about 2,500 years ago by mound-building Native Americans that built the complex that now forms the *Crystal River Archeological Site*. The site was occupied for about 3,000 years. It is not known why the complex was abandoned.

• *Tarpon Springs* is known for elaborate religious ceremonies related to the *Greek Orthodox Church*. The most famous is Epiphany, celebrated every January 6 with the blessing of the waters and the boats. The city's population is known to triple in size for that day. The blessings conclude with the ceremonial throwing of a wooden cross into the city's *Spring Bayou*, and boys ages 16 to 18 dive in to retrieve it: whoever recovers the cross is said to be blessed for a full year. Following the blessings, the crowd moves to the *Sponge Docks* for a fiesta of food and music as part of the celebration festivities.

• *North Tampa* residents petitioned the U.S. government for their own post office in 1912, but they were turned down. Then, with the help of *George Sibthorpe*, the *Stemper* postmaster, they petitioned to have the *Stemper Post Office* moved to *North Tampa*. On January 27, 1913, the U.S. Post Office granted their request; however, fearing the name *North Tampa* would be confused with *Tampa*, the department insisted that the new Post Office be named *Lutz*, the name taken from the *Lutz Junction* train depot; the wood stop north of *Stemper*.

• The *Fort Harrison*, the Grande Dame of downtown *Clearwater*, was the springtime home of the *Philadelphia Phillies* baseball team for many years, and later embraced touring entertainers from the *Rolling Stones* in the 1960s, to jazz legends such as *Count Basie* and *Harry James* in the 1970s.

• Long the focal point for downtown *Clearwater*, during *World War II*, the *Fort Harrison* hotel billeted the *588th Army Airborne Squadron*, hosting benefits and shows in aid of the war effort.

• Since 1975, the *Church of Scientology* has been the proud caretaker of *The Fort Harrison* in downtown *Clearwater*. Over the last two decades, the hotel was restored to its original splendor and beyond, from its lobby and restaurants, to well-maintained grounds, the auditorium, cabanas and the stunning Crystal Ballroom.

• The 1.4 billion gallons of hot water flowing through the cooling system of *Big Bend Power Station* on *Tampa Bay* daily could provide every New York City resident with 3 hot showers.

• *Tampa Bay* was the birthplace of commercial airline service, when pioneer aviator *Tony Jannus* flew the inaugural flight of the *St. Petersburg-Tampa Airboat Line* on January 1, 1914, from *St. Petersburg* to *Tampa* using a *Benoist Flying Boat;* the first scheduled commercial airline flight in the world.

• Two botanical gardens are located within *Pinellas County. The Florida Botanical Gardens*, a part of the *Pinewood Cultural Park* in *Largo*, and *Sunken Gardens*, a former tourist attraction located in and now run by the City of *St. Petersburg*.

• *Nick Chillura Nuccio*, a two-time mayor of *Tampa*, in the 1950s and 60s, was the first *Tampa* mayor of "Latin" decent. He was born and reared in the immigrant neighborhood of *Ybor City*, as the son of *Sicilian* immigrants who were among the first to populate *Ybor City*. He died in 1989, and a large bronze statue holding his trademark hat and large Tampa cigar was dedicated in *Ybor City's Centennial Park* in 1999.

• *Vienna Girardi*, winner of ABC's *The Bachelor* visited *Busch Gardens Tampa Bay*, where she hand-fed an endangered 2,800 pound black rhinoceros before coming face-to-face with a *Bengal tiger*. The central Florida native is a graduate of *Seminole High School in Sanford, Florida,* and opened a specialty clothing store in *Orlando* known as *Vixen*.

• *Southwest Airlines* carries the largest share of TIA passengers, operating a peak-season schedule of over 90 daily flights.

• Since 1985, the *Citrus County Historical Society* has been located in *The Old 1912 County Courthouse*, located at 1 Courthouse Square in Inverness. The historic Courthouse was listed on the *National Register of Historic Places* in 1992.

• Since 1982 the *Stringer House* in *Brooksville* has been home to the *Hernando Heritage Museum*. This picturesque 4-story house was built in 1856, on land obtained by *Richard Wiggins* under the Armed Occupation Act in 1843. It gave settlers land provided they stay there and cultivate it for five years. *John May* bought the property in 1855 and the next year he donated 15 acres to the county for the county seat. May lived here until his death in 1858 and his wife continued until her death in 1869. The house was later sold to *Dr. Sheldon Stringer* and later was lived in by *Judge Fred Stringer*. Eventually, the house was sold to *Dr. Earl Hensley* and his wife, *Helen*, who leased it with an option to buy, to the *Hernando Historical Museum Association* in 1981 to house artifacts of *Hernando County*.

Stringer House

• *Joseph Bradford Lancaster* was elected first *Mayor of Tampa* in 1856, but died that same year. Lancaster served on the *Florida Supreme Court* from 1848 to 1850. He was born in Kentucky in 1790, and moved to Florida in the 1820s at the request of former Kentuckian, and the first civilian Governor of the Florida Territory, *William Pope DuVal*.

- *Michael Connelly* of *Tampa* is a prolific writer best known for detective novels and other crime fiction, notably 20 novels featuring *LAPD Detective Hieronymus "Harry" Bosch* and several with criminal defense attorney (Lincoln Lawyer) *Mickey Haller.* His books are translated into 36 languages, and have garnered many awards. A graduate of the *University of Florida*, Connelly was the *President of the Mystery Writers of America* 2003-04.

Michael Connelly

- More than 90 percent of the population of *Citrus County* live outside the only two cities of *Inverness* and *Crystal River.*

- *Robert "Bob" Martinez*, a long-time *Democrat*, changed his affiliation to *Republican* in 1983, and in 1986, he resigned as *Mayor of Tampa* to run for governor. He won, to become the *second Republican* elected to that office since Reconstruction and the *first Hispanic* to serve as *governor of Florida*.

- *Tampa International Airport* is a major public airport located six nautical miles west of the central business district of *Tampa*, in *Hillsborough County*. This airport is publicly owned by *Hillsborough County Aviation Authority*.

- The *people mover* system at *Tampa International Airport* was the first such system in the world. The original eight trains were built by *Westinghouse*.

- *Tampa Bay* is the largest open-water estuary in *Florida*. The bay encompasses nearly 400 square miles and borders three counties; *Hillsborough, Manatee* and *Pinellas*. The sprawling watershed for *Tampa Bay* covers a land area nearly five times as large, at 2,200 square miles.

• More than 100 tributaries flow into *Tampa Bay*, including dozens of meandering, brackish-water creeks and four major rivers - the *Hillsborough, Alafia, Manatee* and *Little Manatee*.

• *Robin Hibbard*, an *MTV Real Worlder*, is from *Tampa*. Before leaving for *The Real World: San Diego*, *Robin* worked as a bartender at *Coyote Ugly Saloon* in *Tampa*. The *San Diego* season premiered in 2004, and was the fourteenth season of the series, which focuses on a group of diverse strangers living together for several months in a different city each season, as cameras follow their lives and interpersonal relationships. First broadcast in 1992, the show is the longest-running program in MTV history, consistently ranking as a top-rated cable series among viewers 12–34 years old. As of Season 27, a total of 201 cast members had appeared on the show.

• *Pinellas County* is a 600 square-mile peninsula protruding from *Florida* like a thumb in *Tampa Bay*. More than half the area, 327 square miles is covered with water. The county contains: 115 Bridges, 35 Miles of Sandy Beaches, 587.77 Miles of Coastline, 52 Golf Courses and 623 Tennis Courts.

• *Bubba Sparxxx (Warren Anderson Mathis)* signed a recording contract with *Virgin Records* in 2004; released *The Charm* with singles *"Ms. New Booty"* and *"Heat It Up"*. He then left *Virgin* to establish his own label. The chunky-style rapper moved to *Tampa* to run *Twice on Sunday Studio*, and start his label.

• After leaving the governor's office in 1991, *Robert Martinez* of *Tampa* was appointed by *President George H. W. Bush* to the cabinet rank position of *Director of the Office of National Drug Control Policy (Drug Czar)* where he served until 1993.

• Three hurricanes *(Charley, Frances, and Jeanne)* hit *Cypress Gardens* in 2004 during the renovation by *Adventure Parks Group*, causing several delays. *Cypress Gardens Adventure Park* finally opened in November 2004. A new attraction, the *Triple Hurricane* roller coaster, was named for the tumultuous storm season. However, in September 2006, *Adventure Parks Group* filed bankruptcy because of $30 million in damages sustained by the 2004 hurricanes that insurance did not cover.

• Counties adjacent to *Pinellas County* are *Pasco* to the north and *Hillsborough* to the east and south. *Manatee County* is directly to the south of *Pinellas* across the mouth of *Tampa Bay*; however, no portion of the two counties actually touch, as *Hillsborough County* controls the channel into *Tampa Bay* and the center span of the *Sunshine Skyway Bridge* linking the two.

• *Barrier islands* and passes for *Pinellas County* include *Anclote Key* off the shore of *Tarpon Springs* and the northernmost point in the county; *Howard Park*, a man-made pocket beach created in the 1960s; *Three Rooker Bar*, the most geologically recent of the barrier islands; *Honeymoon Island; Hurricane Pass; Caladesi Island; Dunedin Pass*, shoaled and closed in the 1980s, linking *Caladesi Island* and *Clearwater Beach; Clearwater Beach; Clearwater Pass; Sand Key*, the longest of Pinellas' barrier islands; *John's Pass; Treasure Island; Blind Pass; Long Key (St. Pete Beach); Pass-a-Grille Channel; Shell Key; Tierra Verde*, on the bay side of *Shell Key*, links the mainland to *Ft. De Soto*. It was created by a dredge-and-fill project that merged several smaller Keys, including *Cabbage and Pine Keys; Bunces Pass; and Mullet Key*, home to *Ft. De Soto* and the southernmost point in the county.

• *Dunedin* is home to the *Dunedin Brewery, Florida's* oldest microbrewery.

• *James Spencer Courier, Jr.* is a former world number one professional tennis player from *Dade City in Pasco County*. During his career, he won four *Grand Slam* singles titles, two at the *French Open* and two at the *Australian Open*. He holds the record for being the youngest man to have reached the finals of all four *Grand Slam* singles tournaments, at the age of 22. He also won five *Masters 1000* series titles.

• Every October, *Busch Gardens* is transformed into *Howl-O-Scream*. This event contains haunted houses, scare zones, and shows. *Howl-O-Scream* is one of the top rated Halloween events in the US. It features some attractions of the park turned into "horrified" nighttime attractions, like *Curiosity Caverns* being turned into *Dark Cavern*.

93

• There are numerous parks and protected areas located in *Pinellas County*, including *Honeymoon Island State Park; Caladesi Island State Park; Anclote Key Preserve State Park; Anderson Park*, Tarpon Springs; *Boca Ciega Millennium Park*, Seminole; *John Chesnut Sr. Park*, Palm Harbor; *Eagle Lake Park*, Largo; *Fort De Soto Park*, Tierra Verde; *Fred Howard Park*, Tarpon Springs; *Lake Seminole Park*, Seminole; *Philippe Park*, Safety Harbor; *Ridgecrest Park*, Largo; *Sand Key Park*, Clearwater; *Sawgrass Lake Park*, St. Petersburg; *John S. Taylor Park*, Largo; *Wall Springs Park*, Palm Harbor; *War Veterans Memorial Park*, St. Petersburg; *Walsingham Park*, Largo; *Brooker Creek Preserve; Mobbly Bayou Preserve; Shell Key Preserve; Weedon Island Preserve and Boyd Hill Nature Preserve*, on the shores of *Lake Maggiore* in south *St. Pete.*

• *St. Petersburg* boasts of home to seven distinctively different museums. Six are located in downtown *St. Petersburg: The Museum of Fine Arts* near the Pier; *Salvador Dali Museum; Florida International Museum* at St. Petersburg College; *Florida Holocaust Museum; Morean Arts Center; Dr. Carter G. Woodson African American Museum;* and the *Leepa-Rattner Museum of Art* is located in *Tarpon Springs*, on the Campus of *St. Petersburg College*.

• In 1887 *Tarpon Springs* became first incorporated city in the area known then as West Hillsborough.

• The first *'Bollywood Oscars'* celebration in the United States was held in Tampa. The IIFA's 15th annual Weekend & Awards was held April 24-26, 2014. The India International Film Association awards weekend included events focused on Indian film, fashion, music, business and culture. It drew well over 30,000 visitors to the bay area. Every year, IIFA takes its awards weekend to a different country. This was the first time it was held in the United States.

• *USF St. Petersburg* was established in 1965 as the *Bayboro Campus.* In 2006, *USF St. Petersburg* was accredited as a separate entity within the *University of South Florida* system by the *Southern Association of Colleges and Schools*.

94

• *Tampa Bay* is very "Hollywood friendly" and has been location for many major movies. Movies filmed or set specifically in *Pinellas County* include: *Spring Breakers* (2013); *Sunlight Jr.* (2012); *Magic Mike* (2012); *Dolphin Tale* (2011), filmed and set at the *Clearwater Marine Aquarium; Immortal Island* (2011); *A Fonder Heart* (2011), several scenes were filmed in *Clearwater;*

Misconceptions (2008), filmed at *Eckerd College; Grace is Gone* (2007), filmed at *Fort De Soto; The Punisher* (2004), filmed at *Fort De Soto* and the *Sunshine Skyway Bridge; American Outlaws* (2001), filmed at *Fort De Soto; Ocean's Eleven* (2001), scene filmed at the *Derby Lane Greyhound Track* in *St. Petersburg; Great Expectations* (1998), filmed at *Fort De Soto Park; Lethal Weapon 3* (1992), scenes filmed at the *Sereno Hotel* (now gone) in *St. Petersburg; Cocoon* (1985), was both filmed and set in *St. Petersburg;*

Thomas Jane - *The Punisher*

Summer Rental (1985), filmed in *St. Pete Beach; Once Upon a Time in America* (1984), filmed at the *Don Cesar hotel on St. Pete Beach; Porky's* (1982), was based on 1960s occurrences at *Boca Ciega High School* and filmed in *Gulfport.*

• *Ybor City* is one of the three *National Historic Landmark Districts* located in *Florida*. Cobblestone streets and huge old cigar factory buildings make up this historic and legendary town. Founded in 1886 by *Vicente Martinez Ybor*, it became *"the cigar capital of the world"* by 1900. The factories were worked by mostly Cuban cigar makers, and to a lesser degree by Italians and Spaniards. By the early 1950s the cigar factories were gone, but *Ybor* was revitalized in the late 1990s and now attracts large numbers of visitors due to the wide variety of shops, restaurants, clubs, and galleries.

• In 1965, *Busch Gardens* opened its *Serengeti Plain* animal habitat, the first of its kind to offer animals in a free-roaming environment. Over the years, the habitat has expanded from a 29-acre to 65-acre area. It is home to the zebra, addra gazelle, reticulated giraffe, bongo, addax, eland, impala, marabou stork, ostrich, East African crowned crane and sacred ibis.

• Opened in 2008, *Jungala* is a 4-acre family attraction that features up-close animal encounters, rope bridges to explore three stories of jungle life, and a water-play area for children. *Jungle Flyers*, a zip line that offers three different flight patterns above the treetops is also located in this area.

• Eleven stories in height, the *Fort Harrison* in downtown *Clearwater* is outlined for miles up and down the coast. The balconied roof gardens overlook the islands and waters of *Clearwater Bay* and the *Gulf of Mexico*.

• The *Tampa Bay Performing Arts Center* is the largest theater complex south the *Mason Dixon* line and *Tampa Convention Center* is one of the largest in the Southeastern United States.

• More than 200 species of fish are found in *Tampa Bay*, including the popular *snook, redfish* and *spotted sea trout*.

• *Sarah Burke*, of *Tampa,* was a *Real World* cast member the season after *Robin's* appearance. The *Philadelphia* installment began filming in April 2004, and premiered September 7 later that year. *Sarah* was working 9-to-5 at a law firm, and planned to attend *University of Florida School of Law*.

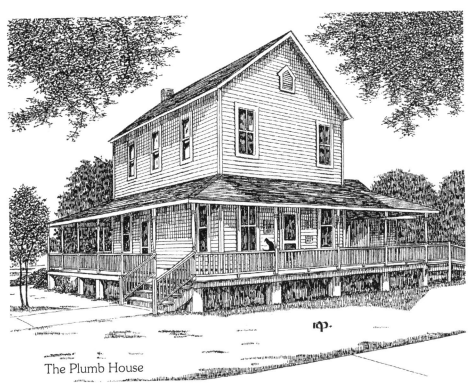

The Plumb House

• The **Plumb House** at 1380 South Martin Luther King Jr. Ave. in Clearwater is headquarters for the *Clearwater Historical Society* and *Plumb House Museum*. It was built in 1896 for use as a store on *South Ft. Harrison* when the *Biltmore* opened. It was later rolled on logs up *Lakeview* and situated next to the cemetery to be used as a residence for the Plumb family. The outside stairway was then removed, and one was built inside.

• *Jennie Plumb* taught the first public school in *Clearwater* in the little log Baptist Church where the cemetery is now located. She was followed by her daughter, who was not only a teacher but also became Principal of the *South Ward School*. The Plumb property was purchased by *Dr. Charles Nach* with an agreement which allowed the family to continue living there. In 1983 he donated it to the *Clearwater Historical Society* as a gift in memory of *Dr. & Mrs. Robert Nach and Lillian Stevens*. To move it to the present location, the mover went west to the railroad and then around the lake. He took this longer route to avoid two main intersections and delicate obstacles.

• In 1823, two years after *Florida* was ceded to the U.S. by Spain, *Dr. Odette Philippe* became the first permanent white settler on the *Pinellas Peninsula. Count Philippe* established a plantation near *Safety Harbor*, which is now *Philippe Park*. He is credited with introducing grapefruit to *Florida* and the U.S.

• *Safety Harbor Resort & Spa* is a 22-acre waterfront landmark on *Old Tampa Bay*. From the first native settlers to the *Tampa Bay* area, people have sought the mineral springs here for rest and renewal. In 1539, *Hernando De Soto* named it *ESPIRIT SANCTU*, meaning "water of the spirits" for the five natural mineral springs he found here. When *Col. William Bailey* was stationed at Fort Brooke in Tampa in the 1850s, he learned of the miraculous springs from the Indians. He bought the land from the U.S. Government and developed it commercially as *Bailey-By-The-Sea*. Each of the five springs boasted cure for a different ailment. In 1917 the town was incorporated as *Safety Harbor,* because it had always been a safe harbor for ships on the bay seeking refuge. The *Safety Harbor Resort & Spa* has long been a favorite for international clients. Today the 50,000 square-foot, world class spa ranks as one a world favorite; one of only twelve in America offering fresh, natural mineral springs.

• During the summer of 2011, the publicly-owned *Tampa Bay Times Forum* underwent a $40 million transformation that was privately funded by *Tampa Bay Sports and Entertainment* owner and chairman, *Jeff Vinik*.

• Actress *Joanna Garcia* of the hit show *Reba* was born in *Tampa*, where she was raised by her father, Cuban-born *Jay Garcia*, a gynecologist, and her mother *Lorraine*, a Spanish-American homemaker and former elementary schoolteacher. She started performing at age 10, and was discovered by the *Disney Channel*, but her parents put school first and she continued to feed her passion by acting in local plays. She was named the homecoming queen at *Tampa Catholic High.* It was while attending *Tampa Catholic High School*, that she was discovered by *Nickelodeon* and starred for three seasons as *Samantha* on *Are You Afraid of the Dark?* She commuted from *Florida* to *Montreal, Canada,* for filming.

Joanna Garcia

• In August 2010 actress *Joanna Garcia* of *Tampa* married *New York Yankees* outfielder *Nick Swisher.* Since her marriage she has changed her stage name to *Joanna Garcia Swisher.*

• *Homosassa Springs State Wildlife Park* is not only a premier attraction, it serves as a refuge for injured and orphaned manatees and as a showcase for native species of animals, plants and fish. At the park entrance, visitors board a pontoon boat from which they may observe raccoons, deer, ospreys, otters and alligators. An underwater observatory gives a close up, spectacular view, of manatees and fish.

• The doors to the 670,000-square-foot *Tampa Bay Times Forum (originally called the Ice Palace)* first opened on October 20, 1996. The first event at the *St. Pete Times Forum* was the *Royal Hanneford Circus;* the first *Lightning* game was played October 20, 1996, a 5-2 win over the *New York Rangers.*

• In 2002, the building was renamed from the *Ice Palace* to the *St. Pete Times Forum* as part of a new partnership with the *St. Petersburg Times.*

• On December 31, 2011 the *St. Petersburg Times* changed its name to the *Tampa Bay Times,* and the arena was unveiled as the *Tampa Bay Times Forum.*

• The massive $40-million transformation in 2011 made history for the *Tampa Bay Times Forum.* The *Forum* hosts more than 150 events ever year, which ranks among the top venues in North America; encompasses 670,000 square feet with three decks and seven separate levels; building is 133 feet 10 inches in height and 493 feet in diameter. It contains 3,400 tons of steel, 30,000 cubic yards of concrete and 70,000 square feet of glass. There are 351 faucets throughout the building and each one is touchless to conserve water.

• The arena, also home to the *Arena Football League's Tampa Bay Storm,* has hosted numerous high-profile events including the *1999 NHL All-Star Game,* the *2007 ACC Men's Basketball Tournament,* the *2008 NCAA Women's Final Four,* the *2009 SEC Men's Basketball Tournament,* a rally for then-presidential candidate *Barack Obama* and host for the *2012 Republican National Convention,* as well as the *2012 NCAA Men's Hockey Championship, the Frozen Four.*

• On average, *Tampa Bay* is only 12 feet deep. Because it is so shallow, manmade shipping channels have been dredged to allow large ships safe passage to the *Port of Tampa.* The main shipping channel, is 43 feet deep and 40 miles long.

• *Lowry Park Zoo* is a 56-acre nonprofit zoo located in *Tampa.* In 2004 it was voted the *#1 Family Friendly Zoo in the U.S.* by *Child Magazine.* It is recognized by the *State of Florida* as the center for Florida wildlife conservation and biodiversity.

• During the 1950s, *Mayor Nick Nuccio* led the push to move *Tampa's* city zoo to a more spacious location. Land further up the river near the neighborhood of *Seminole Heights* was chosen. The combination zoo and park was christened *Lowry Park* in honor of *Gen. Sumter Loper Lowry*, a local resident celebrated for civic contributions and his service in several wars.

• *Lowry Park Zoo* opened in 1957. The zoo shared the park with *Fairyland*, where concrete statues depicted nursery rhymes and fairy tales along a winding maze of paths. This whimsical area was accessible via a large *rainbow bridge*. By the early 1980s, the zoo featured a small roller coaster, a sky ride, and several other kiddie rides, and the wildlife collection had increased dramatically. However, the zoo facilities were in desperate need of repair. After some intensive fundraising and with support of the city, the old zoo was closed in the mid-80s for a complete reconstruction. Nearly all traces of the original zoo (including Fairyland) were removed, and the totally revamped zoo opened in March 1988. *Lowry Park Zoo* in now recognized as the #1 family-friendly Zoo in the United States by *Child* magazine. The *Zoo* features more than 2,000 animals on 56 acres of lush, natural habitats in seven main exhibit areas.

• In 1901, the *Atlantic Coast Line Railroad* took over the *Plant System*, which had numerous lines within *Florida* and *Georgia*. *ACL* operated this turntable at the southern terminus in downtown *St. Petersburg* at *First Street South*. By 1913, the turntable was relocated to *Eleventh Street S.*

• In 1888, a passenger depot was styled by the Russian-born owner of the *Orange Belt Railway*, *St. Petersburg's* first rail line. The *Detroit Hotel*, also built by the railroad, was at the time the only structure within eyesight of the depot.

• The *Port of Tampa* is *Florida's* largest port, seventh largest in the nation, and consistently ranks among the top ten ports across the nation in trade activity. It contributes billions of dollars annually to the region's economy.

• In 2010, the world's second largest theme park and attraction operator *Merlin Entertainments* bought *Cypress Gardens* in *Winter Haven* to use the site for the World's fifth *Legoland* park. The park was converted into *Legoland Florida,* and the new park opened October 15, 2011. The park covers 145 acres of the former *Cypress Gardens*, making *Legoland Florida* the largest *Legoland* park in the world.

• *USF* has operated *WUSF*, an FM radio station since 1963. It offers classical and jazz music and National Public Radio (NPR).

• The first major industry is *St. Petersburg* was born in 1899 when *Henry Hibbs*, a native of *Newport, North Carolina*, started his wholesale fish business at the end of the railroad pier, which extended out to the shipping channel. Within a year, *Hibbs Fish Company* was shipping more than 1,000 pounds of fish daily.

• In the 1980s, book publisher *Harcourt, Brace, Jovanovich* purchased *Cypress Gardens* along with *SeaWorld, Circus World (later rebuilt as Boardwalk & Baseball)* and *Stars Hall of Fame*. They sold most of the businesses to *Anheuser-Busch* in 1989. *Busch* operated *Cypress Gardens* until 1995, when a group of the park's managers led by *Bill Reynolds* bought the property.

• The *Nick Bollettieri Tennis Academy* in *Bradenton*, was founded in 1978 by *Nick Bollettieri* as a full-time tennis boarding school. It combines intensive tennis training with an academic curriculum. In 1987, thirty-two students or former students of the *Bollettieri Tennis Academy* were in the *Wimbledon* draw and twenty-seven were in the *US Open*.

• *Clearwater* is the spiritual headquarters of the *Church of Scientology*, and many prominent celebrities have passed through the area for that reason. *Kirstie Alley* and *Lisa Marie Presley* have lived in *Clearwater, John Travolta* owns a ranch in *Ocala*, and Jazz pianist *Chick Corea* is a *Clearwater* resident.

• Original plans for *Oldsmar,* north of *Tampa,* included a golf course and a luxurious hotel on the bay, but neither ever materialized. A sawmill and foundry that made cast-iron engines for tractors and grove heaters became established. The mill produced the *Olds Chair (also called the Oldsmar Chair),* a sturdy pine or cypress chair sold throughout the United States.

• In 1834 much of west central Florida, including the Pinellas peninsula (then known simply as West Hillsborough), was organized as *Hillsborough County.* The very next year *Odet Philippe* became the first permanent, non-native resident of the peninsula when he established a homestead near the site of the Tocobaga village in *Safety Harbor.* It was Philippe who first introduced both citrus culture and cigar-making to Florida.

Claflin House

• The *Claflin House* in *Brooksville* was built from cypress and heart pine shipped from the *Carolinas* in 1908 as a wedding gift from the bride's father to *Theodore Coogler*, a prominent lawyer. The magnificent Greek revival style house is situated on approximately an acre of land, nestled in the very heart of *Brooksville*. It is best known as the home of *County Judge Monroe Treiman,* who moved here in the early 60s. *Keith and Linda Claflin* purchased the 4,000 square foot house in 1988. They restored it, and opened it as a Bed-&-Breakfast.

• *Coastal Heritage Museum* in *Citrus County* is housed in the 1939 *Crystal River* city hall.

• The town of *Homosassa* in *Citrus County* is home of the *Yulee Sugar Mill State Park, Homosassa Springs State Wildlife Park,* and *Old Homosassa*, a delightful fishing village. The area has been considered a sports lover's paradise since the turn of the century, frequented by prominent Americans such as *Grover Cleveland, Thomas Edison,* and *Winslow Homer*.

• *St. Petersburg's Water Reclamation System* is not only the first to be built in the U.S., it remains one of the largest in the world. The city's innovative system provides more than 20 million gallons a day (annual average) to 10,483 customers.

• *Tampa International Airport* serves 72 non-stop destinations, including international service to *Canada, Mexico, Switzerland,* the *United Kingdom*, and places throughout the *Caribbean*.

• Before hooking up with *David Crosby, Graham Nash* and *Neil Young, Stephen Stills,* the man who put the S in *CSN (Crosby, Stills & Nash)* attended *Plant High School* in *Tampa*. As a child he developed an interest in blues and folk music, and was also influenced by the Latin sound. He also attended *Admiral Farragut Academy* in *St. Petersburg*, as well as *Saint Leo College Preparatory School* in Saint Leo, Florida. *Stephen Stills* attended *LSU*, but dropped out to pursue a music career in the early 1960s. Stills became the first person to be inducted twice on the same night into the *Rock and Roll Hall of Fame* for his work with *CSN* and with the *Buffalo Springfield*.

Stephen Stills

• Mangrove-blanketed islands in *Tampa Bay* support the most diverse waterbird nesting colonies in North America, annually hosting 40,000 pairs of 25 different species of birds, from the familiar white ibis and great blue heron to the regal reddish egret, the rarest heron in the nation.

• The *Vinoy Renaissance St. Petersburg Resort & Golf Club* in downtown *St. Petersburg*, illustrates exquisite *Mediterranean Revival* architecture. Construction for the originally named *Vinoy Park Hotel* began on February 5, 1925.

Vinoy Renaissance

• The contractor set a record for completing the 375-room *Vinoy Park Hotel* in just under 10 months, in time for a grand opening on New Year's Eve 1925. It quickly became one of the country's most prestigious and coveted getaways.

• *Vinoy Park Hotel* has seen several transformations including use as a housing and training center for military cooks and bakers. The property stood unoccupied for 18 years and then underwent a $93 million reconstruction in 1990. Restored to its original grandeur, it soon regained its prominence as a jewel of St. Petersburg's downtown waterfront and has earned a National Register of Historic Places designation.

• *Masaryk Restaurant* stands as a dignified landmark of the community founded by the *Hernando Plantation Company* in the 1920s. *Joseph Joscak*, editor of the *New Yorksky Dennik*, a daily *Slovak* newspaper, dreamed of a "paradise" in *Florida*. He and friends formed a corporation of 60 *Slovaks* and *Czech, Milan Getting*, *Czechoslovak Consul*. They selected an area 10 miles south of *Brooksville*, and each of the 135 shareholders received 20 acres of land. *Masaryktown* was selected as the name to honor *Thomas Masaryk*, first president of the newly created *Czechoslovakia*. The settlers built a school, established a farming co-op and developed a well-planned town, but barely survived two severe winters. Several families returned north, but an eventual break in fortunes helped create a very prosperous community for those who endured.

Masaryk Restaurant

• Each square meter of *Tampa Bay* sediment contains an average of 10,000 animals; mostly tiny, burrowing worms, crustaceans and other mud-dwellers that are known as benthic invertebrates. The most numerous creature in the bay sediment is a primitive, fish-like invertebrate about two inches long that are called branchiostoma.

• *Fort De Soto Park* is located just outside of *St. Petersburg*. The park, operated by *Pinellas County*, is made up from five offshore keys, or islands at the mouth of *Tampa Bay* on the *Gulf of Mexico: Madelaine Key, St. Jean Key, St. Christopher Key, Bonne Fortune Key* and the main island of *Mullet Key,* which is where the *Quartermaster Storehouse Museum* is located. Today all are connected by land to each other. The island group is accessible by toll road from the mainland.

• *Battery Laidley* was the primary defense and *Battery Bigelow* was secondary defense for *Fort De Soto*. Even though **Battery Bigelow** was totally destroyed by the hurricane of 1921, the *Fort De Soto* batteries were both placed on the *National Register of Historic Places* in 1977. Visitors can walk through *Battery Laidley,* home to the last four surviving carriage-mounted 12-inch seacoast mortars in the continental United States.

12-inch M1890 M-1 mortars
Fort DeSoto Park

Carole Baskin, founder and CEO of Big Cat Rescue, Tampa

- *Big Cat Rescue* is the largest accredited sanctuary in the world dedicated to abused and abandoned big cats. Situated on 55 acres in the *Citrus Park* area of north *Tampa*, it is home to over 100 lions, tigers, bobcats, cougars and other species. Their mission is to provide a safe home for the cats as well as to educate the public about the plight of these majestic animals, to end abuse and avoid extinction.

- *Big Cat Rescue* in *Tampa* began rescuing exotic cats in 1992. Big Cat Rescue has 14 species of cats, many of whom are threatened, endangered or extinct now in the wild, including: Tigers, Lions, Leopards, Cougars, Bobcats, Servals, Ocelots, Caracals, Lynx, Jungle Cats, and a Geoffroy Cat.

- A number of big name celebrities have been a part of *Big Cat Rescue* in some way. They include: *Bo Derek, Harrison Ford, Leonardo DeCaprio, Jane Goodall, Kate Walsh, Jack Harris, Barbara Niven, Jim Fowler, Jack Hanna, Bill Murphy, Tippi Hedren, Tim Harrison, Arch Deal, Congresswoman Castor, &* athletes from the *Tampa Bay Bucs, Lightning, & NY Yankees.*

• A year-round top vacation spot, *Clearwater* offers virtually an endless supply of sun with award winning beaches. It is ideally situated on the *Gulf of Mexico* on *Florida's* west coast, and boasts such awards as *Best City Beach*, one of *America's Top Family Beaches*, one of the *Top Singles Beaches in Florida*, and one of the *Best Beaches from Maine to Hawaii.*

• *"Macho Man" Randy Savage* died of a sudden heart attack while driving with his wife, *Barbara Lynn Payne*, in *Seminole, Florida* on a May morning in 2011. *Randall Mario Poffo*, better known as *"Macho Man"* was a professional wrestler, who held twenty championships during his career. Before wrestling he was a professional baseball player. *Randy Poffo* played his last season in 1974, for the *Tampa Tarpons*. He broke into the wrestling business in 1973 during the fall and winter of the baseball off season, and was convinced to change his ring name to *Randy Savage* by a promoter who said 'Poffo' just didn't suit a man "who fights like a savage." He was billed from *Sarasota*, but actually made his residence in *Treasure Island* in the *Pinellas County* side of *Tampa Bay.*

• *Gator Falls* at *Lowry Park Zoo* in *Tampa*, opened in 2008. It is a log flume ride that features a single 30-foot drop, and carries riders over the *albino alligator exhibit*. These are two of only 38 known white gators in the world. There are none in the wild, because they are too flashy and not camouflaged.

• *Indian Shores* is home to the *Suncoast Seabird Sanctuary*, currently the largest non-profit wild bird hospital in the United States and considered one of the top avian rehabilitation centers in the world. A variety of species can be found at the sanctuary. It is open 365 days a year and is free to the public.

• *Tarpon Springs* was incorporated as a city in 1887, and in 1888 the *Orange Belt Railway* was extended into the southern portion of the peninsula. Railroad owner *Peter Demens* named the town that grew near the railroad's terminus *St. Petersburg* in honor of his hometown. The town would incorporate in 1892. Other major towns in the county incorporated during this time were *Clearwater* (1891), *Dunedin* (1899), and *Largo* (1905).

Posey House

- *The Posey House* is located on the *Gulf of Mexico*, in *Hernando County*, near *Aripeka*. It is situated in the center of a 5-acre island. This impressive Victorian house rests quietly beneath clusters of palm, oak and pine trees. It was built circa 1885 by *E. G. Willingham*, an English lumber baron who lived in Atlanta. He and his family used this for their winter retreat until he retired in 1910. His widow sold the estate in 1939.

- The *American Victory Mariners Memorial & Museum Ship* is a unique and innovative maritime attraction aboard the *World War II* era merchant ship *SS American Victory*. Located near downtown *Tampa* and adjacent to the *Florida Aquarium*, the memorial creates a world-class museum depicting life aboard merchant ships during *World War II* and the *Korean* and *Vietnam* conflicts. The museum presents maritime artifacts and multimedia exhibits describing life at sea and the role of *Tampa Bay's* maritime industry in worldwide commerce.

- The first president of *USF, John Allen*, served 1957-1970. Under his leadership, the *University of South Florida* touted itself as the *"Harvard of the South."* *USF* became the first new institution of its kind to be conceived, planned and built in the United States in the 20th century.

• *The Lowry Park Zoo* in *Tampa* features a larger collection of *Florida* species than any other zoo; including Key Deer, American Alligator, Flamingos, Roseate Spoonbill, Florida Panther, American Crocodile, North American River Otter and many other species. The zoo also features several hands-on exhibits, including Lorikeet feeding, stingray feeding, camel rides, an interactive discovery center, a petting area, a river eco-tour and West Indian Manatee encounters. The zoo also features African elephants, giraffe, zebra, White Rhinoceros, shoebill stork, okapi, meerkats and other African species.

• A pair of white tiger cubs, a boy and a girl, were born at *Tampa's Lowry Park Zoo;* the second litter for mom *Nikki* while living at the *Lowry Park Zoo.* White tigers originate from Bengal tigers. They are not albinos and not a separate subspecies of tiger.

• The *Pinellas County School System* is the 7th largest district in *Florida;* 22nd largest in the nation. There are nearly 150,000 students enrolled at 140 public schools, 72 private schools and 5 vocational/technical schools.

• *Sunken Gardens* is a botanical paradise in the very center of a bustling city. As *St. Petersburg's* oldest living museum, this 100 year old garden is home to some of the oldest tropical plants in the region. It includes paths, lush with exotic plants from around the world, cascading waterfalls and more than 50,000 tropical plants and flowers.

• The *University of Tampa* fielded a men's football team from 1933 to 1974, and was the original team playing in *Tampa Stadium*. The team officially moved to Division I in 1971 and defeated the *Miami Hurricanes* in 1970 and 1972. Several of players went to the NFL, and it won the *Tangerine Bowl*. The lagging attendance caused the university to lose money on the program, and it was terminated at the end of the 1974 season.

• *St. Nicholas Greek Orthodox Cathedral* in *Tarpon Springs* is patterned after *St. Sofia's* in *Constantinople*. This church is an excellent example of New Byzantine architecture with an interior of sculptured Grecian marble, elaborate icons and stained glass. The Cathedral was built in 1943, replacing a smaller structure built in 1907 by early Greek settlers.

• In 1824, only two months after arrival of the first American settler into the area, four companies of the U. S. Army established *Fort Brooke* to protect the strategic harbor at *Tampa Bay*. Development of the *Tampa Bay* region began after the Florida territory became part of the U.S. in 1845.

• Former *U.S. Representative* **Sam Gibbons** was instrumental in the creation of *USF*, and is considered to be the school's founder. It was built on the site of *Henderson Air Field*, a *World War II* airstrip. Although located in **west-central Florida**, at the time of its establishment *USF* was the southernmost public university in the state of *Florida*, a situation that gave *University of South Florida* its sometimes confusing name.

• A single quart of *Tampa Bay* water may contain as many as 1 million phytoplankton; microscopic, single-celled plants that are an essential thread in the "who eats who" marine food web.

• The *Tampa Municipal Museum* was established by the city to preserve the hotel in its original form and co-exist with the newly established *University of Tampa*. In 1941, the city of *Tampa*

signed a 99 year lease with the *University*. In 1974, the *Tampa Municipal Museum* was renamed the *Henry B. Plant Museum*.

•The *Henry B. Plant Museum* is housed in the south wing of the former *Tampa Bay Hotel*. The museum displays furnishings and gilded art original to the hotel. Exhibits trace the history of the hotel and the *Tampa Bay* area. The hotel was built in 1891 by *Henry B. Plant*, the transportation magnate who was instrumental in the

Henry B. Plant

reconstruction of the south. *Plant* built eight hotels along his railroads, but this lavish resort was by far his most prized. The building served as the headquarters for *Theodore Roosevelt* in the *Spanish-American War*.

114

USF Marshall Center Running of the Bulls

• The *Marshall Center* (originally called the University Center) was built in 1959 and opened in 1960. The *University Center* was one of the first five buildings that comprised the *University of South Florida* campus when the campus opened in 1960. *Phyllis P. Marshall* served as director from August 1976 to her retirement in June 1994. After years of student lobbying, on March 3, 1994, the *University Center* was renamed in her honor. The *Marshall Center* is the largest university student center in the state of *Florida*.

• The *University of South Florida System* has four institutions: the primary *Tampa* campus, *USF St. Petersburg*, *USF Sarasota -Manatee* and *USF Polytechnic*. There is also a center in *downtown Tampa*. A fourth satellite campus, in *Fort Myers*, was in operation from 1974 until 1997. Campus operations were folded into the new *Florida Gulf Coast University*. The *Fort Myers* campus was at the time shared with *Edison College*, and Edison now controls the entire campus.

• *Tampa* is listed in the *Guinness Book of World Records* for the most number of days of sunshine.

115

• In the 1950s the *Atlantic Coast Line* diesel passenger trains backed into the *St. Petersburg* depot along First Avenue S. All the Track was removed in 1960s and the area is now near the southernmost part of the *Pinellas Trail.*

• *St. Armands Circle* is the center focus of *St. Armands Key,* just across the *Ringling Causeway* from *Sarasota.* This was a mangrove island, purchased in 1893 by Charles St. Amand. In later deeds his name was misspelled *"St. Armand"* and this spelling persisted. Circus magnate *John Ringling* purchased the property in 1917 and planned a development which included residential lots and a shopping center laid out in a circle. Since there was no bridge, he used an old paddle-wheel steamboat to service the island. In 1925 he started the *Ringling Causeway,* and used elephants to transport timbers for the bridge. One year later he led his Circus Band across the causeway to open the *Ringling Estates* with great pomp and circumstance, and offered free bus service to downtown *Sarasota* every hour. In 1928 he gave the causeway and bridge to the city. The circular walk which surrounds the area where *Ringling* first built his bandstand proudly features bronze plaques to commemorate circus stars from the golden era of entertainment.

• Prominent *Tampa* attorney *Brad Culpepper* and his wife *Monica* were contestants on the *CBS* reality show *Survivor: Blood vs. Water* in 2013. *John Broward Culpepper*, nicknamed Brad, was a professional football player in the National Football League (NFL) for nine seasons during the 1990s and early 2000s. Culpepper was an All-American player for the *University of Florida*, and was selected in the 1992 NFL Draft. In his professional career he played for the *Minnesota Vikings, Tampa Bay Buccaneers* and *Chicago Bears.*

• *Monica Culpepper* was originally selected as a participant for the 24th season of the CBS reality television show *Survivor: One World* (2012) from more than 800 applicants. She started in the all-women *Salani* tribe, but soon after being placed in the *Manono* tribe Monica was blindsided in a 5-2 vote in an effort to rid the game of a potential threat. She returned for the 27th season *Blood vs. Water* in 2013 with her husband Brad.

Florida Counties

- There are 67 counties in the state of Florida. It became a territory of the United States in 1821 with two counties complementing the provincial divisions retained as a Spanish territory: *Escambia* to the west and *St. Johns* to the east, divided by the Suwanee River. All of the other counties were apportioned from these two original counties.

- Florida became the 27th U.S. state in 1845, and its last county was created in 1925 with the formation of Gilchrist County from a segment of Alachua County.

Five counties were created in Florida that no longer exist:

- 1. *Benton County* (1844-1850) - Name was changed from Hernando and then changed back to Hernando.

- 2. *Fayette County* (1832-1834) was formed from Jackson and then merged back into Jackson.

- 3. *Mosquito County* (1824-1845) was created in in 1824, and the name was changed to Orange County in 1845.

- 4. *New River County* (1858-1861) - name was changed to Bradford County.

- 5. *Saint Lucia County* (1844-1855) - name changed to Brevard in 1855, then part of Brevard became Saint Lucie County in 1917.

- In 1850 the entire area between Hillsborough County and Levy County was named Benton County, for U.S. Sen. Thomas Hart Benton. When he began to speak against slavery, the Florida Legislature changed the county name to Hernando.

Formation of Florida's 67 counties; listed alphabetically.

- *Alachua County* (Gainesville) was formed in 1824 from Duval and St. Johns counties. The name comes from a native word for the watering holes in the area.

- *Baker County* (Macclenny) was formed in 1861 from Bradford County: It was named to honor James McNair Baker.

- *Bay County* (Panama City) was formed in 1913 from Calhoun and Washington Counties: Named for St. Andrew's Bay, the central geographic feature of the county.

- *Bradford County* (Starke) was formed in 1858 from Columbia County. It was called New River County until 1861; renamed for Capt. Richard Bradford.

- *Brevard County* (Titusville) was formed in 1844 from Orange County. It was called St. Lucia County until 1855; renamed for Thomas Washington Brevard, former state comptroller.

- *Broward County* (Fort Lauderdale) was formed in 1915 from Dade and Palm Beach Counties. Named for Napoleon Bonaparte Broward, former governor of Florida.

- *Calhoun County* (Blountstown) was formed in 1838 from Franklin, Jackson, and Washington Counties: Named for President John C. Calhoun.

- *Charlotte County* (Punta Gorda) was formed in 1921 from DeSoto County. Named for Queen Charlotte Sophia, wife of King George III.

- *Citrus County* (Inverness) was formed in 1887 from Hernando County. Named for the county's numerous citrus trees.

- *Clay County* (Green Cove Springs) was formed in 1858 from Duval County. Named in honor of the great statesman Henry Clay who had died just a few years earlier.

- *Collier County* (East Naples) was formed in 1923 from Lee County. It was named for Advertising mogul Barron Collier.

- *Columbia County* (Lake City) was formed in 1832 from Alachua County. It was named to honor Christopher Columbus.

- *DeSoto County* (Arcadia) was formed in 1887 from Manatee County. Named in honor of explorer Hernando de Soto.

- *Dixie County* (Cross City) was formed in 1921 from Lafayette County. Dixie is a common nickname for the Southern states.

- *Duval County* (Jacksonville) was formed in 1822 from St. Johns County. The county was named in honor of William Pope Duval, former territorial governor.

• *Escambia County* (Pensacola) was formed in 1821. It was one of the two original counties of Florida: From a Creek Indian word meaning "clear water."

• *Flagler County* (Bunnell) was formed in 1917 from St. Johns and Volusia Counties. Named for Henry Morrison Flagler, builder of the Florida East Coast Railway.

• *Franklin County* (Apalachicola) was formed in 1832 from Gadsden and Washington Counties. Named in honor of Benjamin Franklin.

• *Gadsden County* (Quincy) was formed in 1823 from Jackson County. The county was named for James Gadsden, a nineteenth-century politician.

• *Gilchrist County* (Trenton) was formed in 1925 from Alachua County. It was named to honor Albert W. Gilchrist, former governor of Florida.

• *Glades County* (Moore Haven) was formed in 1921 from DeSoto County. Named to honor the Florida Everglades.

• *Gulf County* (Port St. Joe) was formed in 1925 from Calhoun County. It was named after the Gulf of Mexico.

• *Hamilton County* (Jasper) was formed in 1827 from Jefferson County. The county was named to honor U.S. Vice-President Alexander Hamilton.

• *Hardee County* (Wauchula) was formed in 1921 from DeSoto County. It was named for Cary A. Hardee, the sitting governor of Florida at the time.

• *Hendry County* (La Belle) was formed in 1923 from Lee County. It was named to honor Francis A. Hendry, early Floridian pioneer and politician.

• *Hernando County* (Brooksville) was formed in 1843 from Alachua and Hillsborough Counties. It was first named for Hernando de Soto, then changed to Benton County in 1844; and changed back to Hernando in 1850.

• *Highlands County* (Sebring) was formed in 1923 from DeSoto County. So named because of the county's unusual hilly terrain.

- *Hillsborough County* (Tampa) was created in 1834 from Alachua and Monroe Counties. It was named for Wills Hill, the Earl of Hillsborough and British Secretary of State for the American Colonies from 1768-1772.

- *Holmes County* (Bonifay) was formed in 1848 from Jackson and Walton Counties. It was named for Thomas J. Holmes, an early settler in the area.

- *Indian River County* (Vero Beach) was formed in 1925 from St. Lucie County. Named for the Indian River Lagoon, which flows through the county.

- *Jackson County* (Marianna) was formed in 1822 from Escambia County. It was named to honor Andrew Jackson.

- *Jefferson County* (Monticello) was created in 1827 from Leon County. The county was named for Thomas Jefferson, 3rd President of the United States, and the county seat of Monticello, was named after Jefferson's estate.

- *Lafayette County* (Mayo) was formed in 1856 from Madison County. It was named to honor the Marquis de Lafayette, hero of the American Revolution.

- *Lake County* (Tavares) was formed in 1887 from Orange and Sumter Counties. It was so named because of the numerous lakes in the region.

- *Lee County* (Fort Myers) was formed in 1887 from Monroe County, and named to honor Confederate Gen. Robert E. Lee.

- *Leon County* (Tallahassee) was formed in 1824 from Duval & Gadsden Counties. Named for explorer Juan Ponce de León.

- *Levy County* (Bronson) was formed in 1845 from Alachua County. It was named to honor David Levy Yulee, one of the state's original U. S. Senators.

- *Liberty County* (Bristol) was formed in 1855 from Gadsden County. Named as a tribute to the patriotic ideal of Liberty.

- *Madison County* (Madison) was formed in 1827 from Jefferson County. It was named in honor of James Madison, fourth President of the United States.

• *Manatee County* (Bradenton) was formed in 1855 from Hillsborough County. The county was named for The Manatee (sea cow), native to Floridian waters.

• *Marion County* (Ocala) was formed in 1844 from Alachua and Orange Counties. The county was named for Francis Marion, hero of the American Revolution.

• *Martin County* (Stuart) was formed in 1925 from Saint Lucie and Palm Beach Counties. Named for John W. Martin, governor of Florida at time.

• *Miami-Dade County* (Miami) was created in 1836 from Monroe County under the Territorial Act of the United States. The county was named after Major Francis L. Dade, a soldier killed in 1835 in the Second Seminole War. In 1997, voters changed the name of the county from Dade to Miami-Dade to acknowledge the international name recognition of Miami. The City of Miami was named for the local Mayaimi Indian tribe. It is the most populous county in Florida and the seventh most populous county in the United States.

• *Monroe County* (Key West) was formed in 1823 from St. Johns County. It was named for U.S. President James Monroe.

• *Nassau County* (Fernandina Beach) was formed in 1824 from Duval County. Named after the Duchy of Nassau in Germany.

• *Okaloosa County* (Crestview) was formed in 1915 from Santa Rosa and Walton Counties. Name comes from a native word meaning "a pleasant place," "black water", or "beautiful place."

• *Okeechobee County* (Okeechobee) was formed in 1917 from Osceola, Palm Beach, and St. Lucie Counties. It was named for Lake Okeechobee; from the Hitchiti words for "big water."

• *Orange County* (Orlando) was formed in 1824 from St. Johns County. The original name was Mosquito County. It was renamed in 1845 for the county's main product.

• *Osceola County* (Kissimmee) was formed in 1887 from Brevard and Orange Counties. It was named for the famed Seminole fighter Osceola.

- *Palm Beach County* (West Palm Beach) was formed in 1909 from Dade County. It was named for the county's two main geographic features.

- *Pasco County* (Dade City) was formed in 1887 from Hernando County. It was named in honor of Samuel Pasco, one of the U. S. Senators from Florida at the time.

- *Pinellas County* (Clearwater) was created in 1911 from Hillsborough County. The name comes from the Spanish Punta Piñal, or "Point of Pines."

- *Polk County* (Bartow) was formed in 1861 from Brevard and Hillsborough Counties. It was named for James K. Polk, the eleventh U. S. President (1845-49).

- *Putnam County* (Palatka) was formed in 1849 from Alachua and St. Johns Counties. Named for Benjamin A. Putnam, former soldier and Florida legislator.

- *Saint Johns County* (Saint Augustine) was created in 1821 as one of the two original counties. It was named in honor of Saint John the Baptist.

- *Saint Lucie County* (Fort Pierce) was formed in 1917 from Brevard County. It was named for Lucia of Syracuse, also known as Saint Lucy.

- *Santa Rosa County* (Milton) was formed in 1842 from Escambia County. It was named for Santa Rosa Island, which was named for Saint Rose of Lima, first Catholic Saint of the Americas.

- *Sarasota County* (Sarasota) was formed in 1921 from Manatee County. The reason for the name is not documented; however. historians believe it was named for either a Calusa word meaning "point of rocks" or "place of the dance," or possibly for Sara de Soto, daughter of Hernando de Soto, who explored the area.

- *Seminole County* (Sanford) was formed in 1913 from Orange County. It was named after the Seminole tribe who desperately fought to hold the area.

• *Sumter County* (Bushnell) was formed in 1853 from Marion County. It was named for Thomas Sumter, a famous general in the American Revolution.

• *Suwannee County* (Live Oak) was formed in 1858 from Columbia County. It was named after the Suwannee River, which is either a corruption of San Juan or a Cherokee word which translates to "echo river."

• *Taylor County* (Perry) was formed in 1856 from Madison County. It was named to honor Zachary Taylor, military hero and twelfth President of the United States. In 1817 Andrew Jackson led an invasion of the Floridas, an incident known as the First Seminole War.

• *Union County* (Lake Butler) was formed in 1921 from Bradford County. It was named to pay tribute to the Northern forces in the American Civil War.

• *Volusia County* (De Land) was formed in 1854 from Orange County. It was named after the largest community at the time, the port of Volusia, whose etymology is unknown.

• *Wakulla County* (Crawfordville) was formed in 1843 from Leon County. It was named after the Wakulla River, named for a Spanish corruption of a Timucuan word.

• *Walton County* (DeFuniak Springs) was formed in 1824 from Escambia and Jackson Counties. Named for George Walton, first Secretary of Florida Territory.

• *Washington County* (Chipley) was formed in 1825 from Jackson and Walton Counties. It was named for George Washington, the first U. S. President.

County Map for Florida

This map of the state of Florida shows the outline of the 67 counties and the year each county was formed.

58587563R00071